Linguistic Disadvantage in Jury Trials

To my father, whose memory inspires me every day, and to my mother, whose love I cherish. May she stay healthy and happy for many more years to come.

LINGUISTIC DISADVANTAGE IN JURY TRIALS

LESSONS FROM HONG KONG AND BEYOND

Eva N. S. Ng

EDINBURGH
University Press

Edinburgh University Press is one of the leading university presses in the UK. Publishing new research in the arts and humanities, EUP connects people and ideas to inspire creative thinking, open new perspectives and shape the world we live in. For more information, visit www.edinburghuniversitypress.com.

Edinburgh University Press Ltd
13 Infirmary Street
Edinburgh EH1 1LT

Typeset in Ehrhardt MT
by Cheshire Typesetting Ltd, Cuddington, Cheshire, and
Printed and bound in the UK using 100% Renewable Electricity by
CPI Group (UK) Ltd

A CIP record for this book is available from the British Library

ISBN 978 1 3995 1069 1 (hardback)
ISBN 978 1 3995 1071 4 (webready PDF)
ISBN 978 1 3995 1072 1 (epub)

Edinburgh University Press acknowledges the generous support of the Harvard-Yenching Institute for the award of a grant to subsidise the publication of this book. We extend our gratitude to the Institute for its commitment to advancing scholarly work and fostering the dissemination of research in the humanities.

EU Authorised Representative:
Easy Access System Europe
Mustamäe tee 50, 10621 Tallinn, Estonia
gpsr.requests@easproject.com

MIX
Paper | Supporting responsible forestry
FSC www.fsc.org
FSC® C013604

This book is printed using paper from well-managed forests, recycling and other controlled sources

Contents

List of figures

List of tables

Preface

Having worked as a full-time interpreter in the courts of Hong Kong before transitioning into academia, I have gained first-hand experience with courtroom discourse and communication during court proceedings. As a novice interpreter fresh out of a university translation programme, I often found myself grappling with the intricacies of language use in the courtroom. I was acutely aware of my own limitations in navigating the day-to-day interactions between legal personnel and lay participants. It was only after months of on-the-job training and exposure to various court proceedings that my competence and confidence began to grow.

Apart from the challenges of language use, the manner in which interlocutors communicated posed an additional obstacle. There were witnesses whose testimony was incoherent or illogical, rendering it difficult to comprehend. Legal professionals sometimes mumbled or rushed their speech, articulating their words as if they were merely murmuring to themselves. This often rendered clarifications with the speakers inevitable.

I recall working for several months with a soft-spoken British judge whose speech was challenging for many in the courtroom to hear. However, my proximity to him allowed me to hear him, making my role crucial, even for English and Cantonese bilingual counsel who often relied on my Cantonese interpretation of the judge's words in English.

I also had the opportunity of observing more senior colleagues interpreting in court before I made my own debut. In one courtroom that I observed, a New Zealand judge's strong accent and mumbled speech, coupled with his thick moustache, rendered his utterances nearly incomprehensible to everyone in court except his interpreter. The regular interpreter assigned to him had worked with him for many years and was accustomed to his accent and speaking style. Consequently, not only monolingual Cantonese-speaking litigants but also bilingual counsel depended on the interpreter's Cantonese interpretation of the judge's utterances in English.

These experiences have led me to ponder how well jurors, who often serve as silent observers and are mostly L2 English speakers, understand court proceedings held in English. Unlike interlocutors engaged in oral communication, jurors do not have the opportunity to seek clarification from speakers and may not have access to the interpretation provided in court, depending on the mode of interpreting used. These experiences also convinced me that jurors' comprehension issues are not confined to Anglo-American courtrooms, where English is the dominant language of most participants in court. I also recognised that jury comprehension studies should not be restricted to analysing the use of legalese in courtroom discourse, as the manner of speaking is just as crucial as the language used to convey meaning. This aspect of research has long been neglected in existing studies on jury comprehension.

An important step in my evolution as a researcher resulted from obtaining authorised access to the audio recordings of two jury trials from the High Court of Hong Kong. This enabled me to examine a hitherto unexplored bilingual courtroom, where the linguistic dichotomy between English-speaking legal professionals and Cantonese-speaking lay participants renders the interpreting service in English-medium trials a *sine qua non*. Utilising the audio recordings to test potential jurors' comprehension of court proceedings allowed my study to extend beyond conventional textual analyses of legal discourse to include speakers' physical voicing as a significant aspect of speech production that impacts listeners' reception and understanding.

My original plan was to focus solely on the jury participation and comprehension issues in Hong Kong. However, having benefitted from the insights of the two reviewers of my book proposal, I decided to broaden my examination to include English-speaking common law jurisdictions, with a particular emphasis on Hong Kong. My year-long stay in the United States from 2022 to 2023 as a visiting scholar at Harvard University reinforced my belief that while these issues are particularly pertinent in Hong Kong, they are also relevant to linguistically diverse societies, including English-speaking countries with significant numbers of immigrants such as the United States. My day-to-day experience revealed that a significant number of individuals in the United States are not proficient in the English language, and my ethnographic observations in the courts in Boston and in San Francisco demonstrated that court interpreters are often required to facilitate non-English-speaking litigants' participation in court proceedings.

These observations strengthened my argument for the use of interpreters as a means to mitigate linguistic disadvantage in jury trials. This book postulates that linguistic disadvantage in jury trials is manifested in two ways. Firstly, individuals lacking language proficiency are disadvantaged and discriminated against in their right to participate in jury trials, which compromises the principle of trial by peers drawn from a cross-section of the community. Secondly, those eligible for jury service may still struggle with comprehension of courtroom discourse due to intralingual legal-lay communication issues, as demonstrated in existing literature contextualised in Anglo-American courtrooms. The findings of my study reveal a genuine need for juror language assistance in English-medium trials, as L2 jurors in

Hong Kong face both interlingual and intralingual comprehension problems arising from the need to comprehend specialist legal language uttered in a foreign tongue.

To effectively mitigate the linguistic disadvantage in jury trials, this book advocates for ensuring quality interpreting to facilitate the meaningful participation of all those who rely on the service to follow court proceedings. It is important for defendants not only to have the right to trial by jury but also to be tried by well-informed jurors.

I hope this book offers a valuable resource for readers seeking to understand the advantages and challenges of implementing the jury system in the unique linguistic landscape of Hong Kong and in other common law jurisdictions with linguistically diverse populations. This book resulting from an interdisciplinary study is intended for researchers in linguistics, law, translation and interpreting, as well as for practitioners in these fields, including translators, interpreters, legal professionals and policymakers.

Eva Ng
November 2024, Hong Kong

Acknowledgements

I wish to thank the following people and institutions. Without their generous help and support, this book would not have come into being.

First of all, I would like to thank the two Hong Kong High Court Registrars, Madam Queeny Au-yeung and Mr Kim Wan Lung, for allowing me to access the recordings of court proceedings, including the two jury trials that I used for my study. Without their visionary and generous support, this first-ever study using authentic recordings of court proceedings to test potential jurors' comprehension would not have been possible.

My thanks also go to the Research Grants Council (RGC) of the University Grants Council (UGC) of Hong Kong for funding my project on Chinese jurors' ability to understand court proceedings conducted in English, which has culminated in the publication of this book.

I would also like to thank my two colleagues at the University of Hong Kong, Professor Chris Hutton and Professor Janny Leung, for reviewing my book proposal. Their insightful comments and suggestions have greatly contributed to the award of an advance book contract from Edinburgh University Press and subsequently to the publication of this book.

I am indebted to my former colleague in the Faculty of Law at the University of Hong Kong, Vandana Rajwani, for her generous help with my study. I have benefitted a lot from her legal knowledge and expertise in courtroom advocacy. Her passion for work and can-do spirit have always been an inspiration to my academic pursuit over the years.

My special thanks go to the Harvard-Yenching Institute (HYI) for awarding me the prestigious fellowship under the Harvard-Yenching Visiting Scholars Program. This provided me with a precious opportunity to spend 10 months at Harvard University as a visiting scholar from 2022 to 2023. During this time, I was able to focus on writing this book, free from the distractions of work and home. More importantly, it allowed me to conduct ethnographic studies in US courts and incorporate these experiences and observations into the book. I also had the chance to take a course in statistical analysis offered by the Harvard Law School and to apply the knowledge I gained to the analysis of my study results. My time at Harvard University also enabled me to engage in academic exchanges and gain valuable feedback by presenting the findings of this research project. To encourage the publication of high-quality academic monographs by former visiting scholars, the HYI also awarded a generous grant to Edinburgh University Press to facilitate the publication of this book issuing from my research stay at the Institute. I am immensely grateful for their generosity and continued support for my work.

I would also like to thank my mentor and talk discussant at Harvard University, Professor Nicholas Harkness, for his guidance during my visit at Harvard. His perceptive and insightful comments and suggestions have greatly contributed to the paper I subsequently published that constitutes part of this book.

I am thankful to the three anonymous reviewers of my book proposal and the independent reader of the entire book manuscript. This book has been enriched by their judicious comments and suggestions.

My gratitude also extends to the 53 participants of the study detailed in this book. Without their involvement, this book would not have come to fruition.

Last but not least, I would like to thank my family and extended families on both sides for their unwavering support for my academic endeavours throughout the years.

Abbreviations/signs used in this book

Abbreviation	Description
§	section
AAVE	African American Vernacular English
ADA	Americans with Disabilities Act
art.	article
BME	black and minority ethnic
BSL	British Sign Language
c.	chapter (law, UK)
CA	Court of Appeal (HK)
Cap	chapter (law, HK)
CFA	Court of Final Appeal (HK)
CI	consecutive interpreting/interpretation
DC	defence counsel
HREC	Human Research Ethics Committee (HK)
HYI	Harvard-Yenching Institute
Hz	hertz
ICC	International Criminal Court
ICCPR	International Covenant on Civil and Political Rights
IQR	interquartile range
JSSA	Jury Selection and Service Act (US)
L1	first language
L2	second/foreign language
LEP	Limited English Proficiency/Limited English Proficient
LOTE	language other than English
n.d.	no date
NES	non-English speaker/speaking
NM Const.	New Mexico Constitution

Nu	Nunavut (Canada)
PC	prosecution counsel
PW	prosecution witness
Q1	lower/first quartile
Q2	median/second quartile
Q3	upper/third quartile
r.	reign
R.	Regina/Rex
RSO	Revised Statutes of Ontario (Canada)
RGC	Research Grants Council (HK)
RSBC	Revised Statutes of British Columbia (Canada)
RSNWT	Revised Statutes of the Northwest Territories (Canada)
SD	standard deviation
SI	simultaneous interpreting/interpretation
SL	source language
U.S. Const. amend. VI	Sixth Amendment of the US Constitution
USC	US Constitution
UGC	University Grants Council (HK)
v.	versus
W	witness
wpm	words per minute

1

Linguistic Disadvantage and Right to a Fair Trial

Linguistic diversity, disadvantage and discrimination

In her book *Linguistic Diversity and Social Justice*, Piller (2016) contends that linguistic disadvantage and discrimination is a result of linguistic diversity, which is becoming increasingly prevalent due to globalisation and human migration. She argues that linguistic diversity is not neutral, and that it necessarily leads to stratification and the hierarchical organisation of different languages and linguistic repertoires, resulting in inequality and social injustice. Piller discusses the linguistic disadvantage and discrimination facing individuals who do not speak the dominant language in society, and demonstrates how language may be used 'as a means of exclusion, discrimination and disadvantage' (2016: 8). Piller's (2016) study focuses on the language domains of work, education, human security and participation in community life. This book addresses the disadvantage and discrimination encountered by potential jurors who do not speak English or have limited English proficiency. It reviews English-speaking Anglo-American jurisdictions where the dominance of English leads to minority language speakers being excluded from jury service. It has been argued that this is an example of linguistic and racial discrimination, and this will be discussed in detail in Chapter 2.

Linguistic disadvantage and discrimination as a result of colonialism

As explained above, linguistic disadvantage and discrimination can be a result of lack of proficiency in the dominant language in linguistically diverse polities. However, it can also be a result of linguistic prestige arising from colonial rule, during which the language used by the colonising power is accorded higher prestige than the language(s) spoken by the colonised people. It is often the language of administration, law, education and trade, despite not being the dominant language spoken by the majority of the population in the colony. As a result, the linguistic majority who lack proficiency in the more prestigious language are inevitably disadvantaged in education, employment opportunities and participation in various domains in society. The linguistic prestige and official status of the colonial language may continue into the post-colonial era as in the case of Hong Kong, where English has been an official language (and the only one before 1974) despite Cantonese being the dominant language spoken by the general public. Because English has been used in court proceedings since the British colonisation of Hong Kong in the nineteenth century, citizens without sufficient knowledge of English have necessarily been excluded from jury service. On the other hand, those who do meet the English proficiency requirement (measured by their education levels) may still be disadvantaged in their participation in jury service due to potential comprehension problems. This disadvantage can diminish their participation as well as compromising the defendant's right to a fair trial, which is the focus of this book.

Linguistic disadvantage in the legal process

Linguistic disadvantage in the legal process refers to the challenges faced by individuals who come into contact with the criminal justice system but are not conversant with the language used in legal proceedings. This can hinder their ability to understand their rights, obligations and the potential consequences of their actions. As noted by Nakane (2016), minority language speakers' participation in the legal process is often examined in connection with the question of whether language assistance is available to these people to compensate for their disadvantage. In this connection, many studies have explored comprehension issues encountered by non-English-speakers (NES) or individuals with limited English proficiency (LEP) facing criminal charges during police interrogations and in court proceedings. Some of these studies have focused on NES or LEP suspects' understanding of police cautions, known as the Miranda Warning in the United States. Such studies conclude that comprehension problems can lead to suspects waiving their Miranda rights, including the rights to remain silent and to be interviewed in the presence of a lawyer (e.g. Pavlenko 2008, 2021, 2023; Pavlenko et al. 2019, 2020). Other studies suggest that police interrogations of NES or LEP suspects that are conducted without the help of a professional interpreter might result in miscommunication and lack of comprehension between police personnel and suspects or potential witnesses to offences (Brown-Blake & Chambers 2007) or even coerced confessions by suspects (Berk-Seligson 2009). These studies argue that linguistic disadvantage can seriously undermine access to justice.

The use of interpreters is the usual way in which linguistic disadvantage may be mitigated in the legal domain. Nakane's (2010) ethnographic study of the use of interpreters in Japanese criminal courts revealed that interpreters were not consistently used throughout the trials but only employed for high-register legal discourse such as counsel's opening and closing statements and judgments. Testimony by witnesses and defendants from non-Japanese-speaking backgrounds was not interpreted at all. Nakane (2010) contends that this partial use of interpreters presents linguistic problems that may disadvantage defendants and witnesses testifying in Japanese spoken only as a second language. In Nakane's (2010) study, the provision of interpreting services for defendants and witnesses was at the discretion of the court. In Ng's (2020) study, however, some expert witnesses voluntarily waived their right to an interpreter and chose to testify in English of which they apparently did not have a sufficient command, possibly due to the linguistic prestige associated with the use of English in Hong Kong. The study revealed that the Chinese witnesses experienced immense communication problems with counsel, especially during the cross-examination phase, which is antagonistic in nature. It was found that the Chinese witnesses were not able to fully understand counsel's questions, nor to adequately respond to those questions. Ng (2020) argues that this linguistic disadvantage renders the Chinese witnesses more suggestible in that they were more ready to agree to the questions put to them by the counsel in cross-examination. This, as Ng (2020) suggests, can be attributed to the fact that the Chinese witnesses had either misunderstood what had been suggested in those questions or that they feigned comprehension to avoid embarrassment.

Linguistic disadvantage in the legal process can also exacerbate the challenges facing laypersons such as jurors who may struggle to comprehend legal language, as the language of the law has been criticised as 'arcane and archaic, complex and convoluted, pompous and ponderous' (Tiersma 1999: 241). Research on jury comprehension has primarily focused on examining the ability of jurors to comprehend complex jury instructions and technical evidence presented during court proceedings. These studies highlighted how difficulties in jurors' comprehension might undermine the integrity of their decisions, thereby jeopardising the defendant's right to a fair trial. Such studies have largely focused on Anglo-American courts, where jurors usually have a solid command of the English language or where English operates as a societal *lingua franca*. The findings indicated that jurors often struggled with legal terminology and the intricate sentence structures typically found in jury instructions. While the use of legalese has been identified as a significant barrier to comprehension, the influence of speakers' delivery styles on jurors' understanding remains largely unexamined. Furthermore, there is a dearth of research on how jurors with limited proficiency in the trial language, let alone legal language, understand courtroom discourse. This linguistic disadvantage is likely to exacerbate jurors' comprehension issues, potentially leading to unsound and unsafe verdicts. Such outcomes could result in miscarriages of justice or costly retrials, shaking public faith in the jury system.

Jurors may thus labour under the double disadvantage of a lack of legal knowledge and insufficient proficiency in the general language used by the court. Given the crucial role of the jury in the legal process, several important questions arise: How do intralingual and interlingual challenges affect jurors' ability to understand legal discourse and navigate the legal process as fact-finders? What implications does this have for defendants regarding their right to a trial by jury and right to a fair trial? A trial before a misinformed or under-informed jury can effectively deny the right to a jury trial (Ritter 2004). This book aims to explore these critical questions.

Background to the book

This book arises from a three-year funded project which examines a critical yet under-researched aspect of the jury system, namely jurors' ability to understand court proceedings in a second language (L2).[1] This issue is particularly pertinent in post-colonial states and linguistically diverse societies, where randomly selected jurors may not possess a sufficient command of the language used in court. This may be compounded by a lack of knowledge about the law and the specialist legal language employed by lawyers. As linguistic diversity continues to grow due to high levels of human migration and increasing economic globalisation, this problem is becoming increasingly critical.[2]

The need to ensure that jurors selected to sit on a jury possess sufficient proficiency in the language to understand the court proceedings seems perfectly justifiable. However, in a society where a significant proportion of the population does not possess the required language proficiency, the language requirement can be problematic and at odds with the notion of trial by jury. As suggested by Leung (2019: 233), linguistic criteria in jury selection may come into conflict with the fundamental rationale of jury trials. In post-colonial polities such as Hong Kong, the juror language requirement necessarily excludes the majority of the population from the jury pool. As mentioned above, even those who meet the requirement may still struggle to comprehend the court proceedings in a language which they speak as an L2. This book is contextualised in such a linguistic landscape and examines the jury comprehension problem in post-colonial Hong Kong courtrooms as a case study. English trials in the High Court of Hong Kong are routinely argued before local jurors who are selected based on education levels. In reality, these jurors may not possess a sufficient command of English to understand the court proceedings. The study detailed in this book aimed to test potential jurors' comprehension of court proceedings using authentic audio recordings extracted from two jury trials. I was granted rare permission to access these recordings, making it the first jury comprehension study to do so.[3] The use of audio recordings of authentic court proceedings has made it possible for the analysis to go beyond the conventional focus on the language in which the message is encoded, extending the analysis to the manner in which the message is delivered. The study reveals that comprehension problems are not limited to legal terminology; non-legal language can be equally challenging for L2 jurors. The findings of the study also show that the manner in which a message is animated has considerable impact on the comprehension of the listeners, who in this case all speak English as their L2.

This book also addresses the tensions surrounding the random selection of jurors and the need for jurors to have a sufficient command of the language used in trials. These tensions are particularly evident in colonial and post-colonial polities that have inherited the jury system and its language. However, they are also experienced in other common law jurisdictions with a linguistically diverse population. Excluding citizens from jury service based on their linguistic proficiency creates barriers to equal participation and disrupts the fundamental rationale of trial by peers. This book therefore explores the provision of interpretation services to jurors as a way to remove language barriers or mitigate the linguistic disadvantages they would otherwise face.

Language assistance for individuals facing criminal charges

Under the International Covenant on Civil and Political Rights (ICCPR) (United Nations 1966), defendants who do not speak the language used in criminal proceedings are entitled to the free assistance of an interpreter. Interpreting in legal proceedings is thus by and large a default service provided for defendants in criminal proceedings in jurisdictions which have acceded to the ICCPR as a way to mitigate the linguistic disadvantage defendants would otherwise suffer. This is also to ensure defendants' linguistic presence and meaningful participation in the judicial process, and to avoid compromising their right to a fair trial.

This provision is, however, not extended to other participants such as witnesses or jurors in court. Although it is not uncommon for a witness who does not speak the language of the court to testify via an interpreter at the discretion of the court, such guarantees are nonetheless not spelt out either in the ICCPR or in any domestic laws modelled on it. On the other hand, jurors selected to sit in a trial are considered to have satisfied the language requirement and to have a sufficient command of the court language, and therefore interpretation for jurors is deemed unnecessary even in ICCPR-compliant jurisdictions.

It must be noted that the provision of interpretation services for jurors, however, is not without its problems. One such issue is the potential for jurors to access incongruent information due to inaccurate interpretation. Therefore, appeals based on interpretation-related problems and the opinions of the appellate court will be examined and discussed. This book also aims to identify problematic institutional practices in court interpreting and propose recommendations for good practice to improve interpretation accuracy and promote linguistic justice. This book asserts that the jury dilemma can be alleviated through the effective use of court interpreters, provided that the court assumes a fair share of responsibility in ensuring the quality of interpretation.

Structure of the book

The book offers a thorough examination of the jury comprehension problem, combining both an overview and an empirical study that has shed new light on the issue. The initial three chapters examine the notion of linguistic disadvantage in post-colonial and linguistically diverse polities, the principle of trial by jury, jury selection as a means of exclusion and linguistic discrimination, and the issue of jury comprehension in a broader context. The next three chapters focus on Hong Kong. Chapter 4 provides an overview of the implementation of the jury system in Hong Kong and presents its linguistic landscape. This chapter highlights the longstanding reliance of the judicial system on court interpreting, as well as the issue of jury comprehension in both the colonial and post-colonial Hong Kong. Chapter 5 expounds on an empirical study investigating Chinese jurors' comprehension of authentic court proceedings and presents the quantitative results of the study. Chapter 6 provides a qualitative analysis of the study results, focusing on both the discursive voicing and the physical voicing of the courtroom discourse most likely to cause comprehension problems for Chinese jurors. Chapter 7 explores the extension of interpreting services to jurors in English-medium trials, which in the context of Hong Kong can be easily implemented with minimal financial implications. This chapter also examines conflicting appellate opinions about an appeal which contested jurors' access to the interpretation provided for the defendant in a drug trafficking trial. It discusses the implications of the appellate courts' judgments, both for the extension of the existing interpreting service to jurors in need of the service and for the current practice of court interpreting. The concluding chapter summarises this book and evaluates its significance within the international context, given the increasing linguistic diversity in the global community. This chapter reiterates the need for interpreting services to be provided to jurors as a means not only to assist their comprehension of court proceedings but also to promote equal participation and the principle of trial by peers. This final chapter also discusses potential issues associated with the provision of interpreting services for jurors and offers recommendations to improve the current state of court interpreting, with the overarching goal of safeguarding defendants' right to a fair trial and delivering justice for all.

Notes

1. The project entitled 'Jury comprehension: English trials heard by Chinese jurors in the Hong Kong courtroom' was funded by the Research Grants Council (RGC) of the University Grants Committee (UGC) in Hong Kong under the Early Career Scheme (ECS). Project No. 27604417.
2. During a one-year sojourn at Harvard University as a visiting scholar from 2022 to 2023, I discovered that a considerable population in Cambridge and Boston, especially those working in retail shops or as cleaners, had limited proficiency in English. These individuals would likely be unable to effectively participate in jury service due to language barriers.
3. In 2009, I was granted special permission by the then High Court Registrar, Madam Justice Queeny Au-yeung, to access the recordings of nine criminal trials, including two jury trials, for teaching and research purposes. Fresh permission to use the two jury trials for this study was sought in 2017 and was granted by the then High Court Registrar of Hong Kong, Mr Lung Kim Wan.

2

Trial by Jury and Jury Selection: Language Matters

The introductory chapter discussed the concept of linguistic disadvantage in the judicial process and the role of interpreters in ensuring defendants' linguistic presence and meaningful participation in criminal proceedings. This chapter focuses on jury trials and discusses how individuals who do not possess a sufficient command of the language of the court can be disadvantaged and excluded from participating in jury service. It explores the origin and fundamental principle of trial by jury and scrutinises relevant laws governing the selection of jurors in major Anglo-American common law jurisdictions, highlighting the general requirement for jurors to be proficient in English to be eligible for jury service. This chapter also reviews relevant literature that challenges the English-language requirement for jurors, arguing that it compromises defendants' rights to be tried by jurors drawn from a cross-section of the community and creates barriers to equal participation in jury service.

Trial by jury

Trial by jury is a cornerstone of the common law system, whereby ordinary people are drawn from the community to decide collectively on the outcome of a trial, as opposed to a bench trial where the decision is made by a lone judge.

The exact time of the introduction of the jury trial into England has received much discussion by historians. It is widely recognised that trial by jury owes its origin to the Magna Carta, which was a contract between King John and 13 barons and bishops made on 19 June 1215; however, Clark (1923) suggests that it should not be credited as the origin or guarantee of trial by jury. Clark's view about the origin of trial by jury is echoed by McSweeney (2014), who states that the actual guarantee of trial by jury does not exist in the Magna Carta. McSweeney (2014: 139) argues that the common law jury began during the reign of King Henry II (r. 1154–1189) (see also Devlin 1956: 7) about 50 years before the signing of the Magna Carta. He observes that by 1215 when the Magna Carta was issued, 'juries had become the primary way of deciding land cases in the royal courts' (McSweeney 2014: 142). In the meantime, King Henry was experimenting with juries to deal with criminal cases (ibid.: 143).

Other studies likewise argue that the origin of trial by jury precedes the Magna Carta, with some suggesting that the jury concept might have been imported into England after the Norman Conquest in 1066, as the Normans had the practice of gathering a group of local people to tell the truth under oath (Lloyd-Bostock & Thomas 1999: 8; see also Devlin 1956: 6; Horan 2012: 11). Jurors in England in early times acted only as sources of information on local affairs before they were gradually used as adjudicators in both civil and criminal disputes (Lloyd-Bostock & Thomas 1999: 8). Initially jurors were summoned to decide on rival claims based on their prior knowledge about the claims in dispute (Horan 2012: 11; Lloyd-Bostock & Thomas 1999: 8). As time went by, jurors were required to be independent of the case, and in the eighteenth century, jurors with personal knowledge of the disputes had to be excused from serving on the jury (Lloyd-Bostock & Thomas 1999: 8–9). This has since become a fundamental principle of the jury system (Horan 2012). Clark (1923) contends that trial by jury, in the form we know it today, did not exist until nearly a century and a half after the Magna Carta was adopted, and it was not until the fourteenth century that trial by jury as we know it today was established.

Despite the disputed origin of trial by jury, for centuries the Magna Carta has been cited as an important source for the guarantee of a fair trial and trial by jury, with specific reference made to Clause 39, provided below in its original Latin followed by the English translation (Clark 1923: 4):

> *Nullus liber homo capiatur, vel imprisonetur, aut disseisiatur, aut utlagetur, aut exuletur, aut aliquo modo destruatur, nec super eum ibimus, nec super eum mittemus, nisi per legale judicium parium suorum vel per legem terrae.*
>
> No freeman shall be arrested or detained in prison, or deprived of his freehold, or outlawed, or banished, or in any way molested; and we will not set forth against him, nor send against him, unless by the lawful judgment of his peers and by the law of the land.

Although it remains debatable whether '*legale judicium parium*' – 'lawful judgment of his peers', can be equated with 'trial by jury' as we know it today, it is indisputable that this clause serves as an important legal reference for the principles of due process and the protection of individual liberties. As noted by Clark (1923), the aim of the Magna Carta was to restrict the power of King John and to protect the bishops and barons from the king's oppression through the judges he appointed. In other words, Clause 39 mandates that the king delegate part of his judicial power to people who were peers of the barons and bishops, thus preventing King John's domination of the courts. Although the Magna Carta did not institute the jury system in its present form, the underlying political intent of Clause 39 served as inspiration for future generations to recognise the right to a trial by jury as a fundamental safeguard against arbitrary government (Library of Congress, n.d.). The Magna Carta was the first document to establish the principle that all people, including the king, must be subject to the law (Breay & Harrison 2014). The core principles of the Magna Carta are reflected in various constitutional documents worldwide, including the United States Bill of Rights (1791), the Universal Declaration of Human Rights (1948) and the European Convention on Human Rights (1950) (Breay & Harrison 2014).

Whatever its origin, trial by jury has been considered a symbol of freedom and democracy. Lord Devlin (1956: 164) considers trial by jury to be 'more than an instrument of justice and more than one wheel of the constitution: it is the lamp that shows that freedom lives'. Devlin's view about trial by jury has been echoed by many over the years. It is argued that placing ordinary citizens in the judicial decision-making process serves to counterbalance the 'undemocratic characteristics of the judiciary' with 'the most immediate and powerful presence of the people' (Landsman 2002: 880). The jury has complete power over the verdict without having to provide an explanation or justification for the verdict. This, as Lloyd-Bostock and Thomas (1999: 9–10) suggest, allows juries to decide on their verdicts according to conscience in defiance of what is considered to be harsh law, as in jury nullification, which is central to the democratic function of the jury. Abramson (1994: 1) contends that 'no other institution of government rivals the jury in placing power so directly in the hands of citizens' as the jury version of democracy entrusts the people at large with 'the power of government' (Abramson 1994: 2). Chávez (2008: 1) suggests that a jury verdict makes justice a 'community project', as ordinary people from the community directly participate in the judicial process as fact-finders.

Jury selection

As noted above, there are different interpretations of trial by peers in relation to trial by jury. Davies and Edwards (2004) discuss the different interpretations of the concept of 'peers' in relation to jury selection and propose narrower and broader interpretations. The narrower interpretation refers to a jury representing a random section of the community, with every citizen considered as an equal peer; the second interpretation is broader and takes a jury to include representatives of a similar background or social group as the accused – the concept of a person's 'peer group'. Davies and Edwards (2004) conclude that both the United States and the United Kingdom have developed a rather narrow concept of trial by peers in relation to jury selection and embrace the idea that everyone is equal before the law; therefore, random selection is the best way to ensure fairness. In the United Kingdom, the Juries Act 1974 stipulates the random selection of jurors as a way to assure impartiality (Davies & Edwards 2004). Likewise, the Supreme Court of Canada has taken a narrow view of representativeness, focusing on the fairness and randomness of the jury selection process rather than the composition of the jury itself (Davison 2020). Davison (2020) contends that it is important to include jurors with shared experiences and backgrounds with the defendant. He argues that a representative jury serves both symbolic and practical purposes. Symbolically, it helps address concerns of racial or ethnic biases and ensures that justice is seen to be done. Practically, a diverse jury brings different perspectives and life experiences that can influence the assessment of evidence and decision-making in the trial (Davison 2020).

In the United States, the Sixth Amendment of the Constitution, which is considered the constitutional guarantee for the right to trial by jury, does not explicitly assert the right to a jury of one's peers. Instead, the Sixth Amendment entitles the accused to a trial by an impartial jury (US Const. amend. VI):

> In all criminal prosecutions, the accused shall enjoy the right to a speedy and public trial, by an impartial jury of the State and district wherein the crime shall have been committed, which district shall have been previously ascertained by law, and to be informed of the nature and cause of the accusation; to be confronted with the witnesses against him; to have compulsory process for obtaining witnesses in his favor, and to have the Assistance of Counsel for his defence.

An impartial jury has been interpreted by courts to mean an unbiased jury drawn from a fair cross-section of the community (see Chernoff 2016; Gonzales Rose 2014; Johnson 2016). The fair cross-section entitlement has been translated into a statutory right in the federal Jury Selection and Service Act (1968).

It can be argued that in the United States, *voir dire* as a way to eliminate potential jurors' biases makes the selection less random compared with the jury selection in the United Kingdom and its former colonies where the jury system is practised. *Voir dire* is a process in which prospective jurors are questioned in court by attorneys about their backgrounds and potential biases before they are selected to sit on a jury and is currently practised only in the US.[1] Gonzales Rose (2020) points out that prospective jurors who speak English with a heavy accent are often excluded from juries because of the court's concerns about their ability to understand proceedings. She contends that accent discrimination in jury selection violates the principle of equal protection under the Fourteenth and Fifth Amendments, and random selection of jurors from a fair cross-section of the community under the Sixth Amendment. Johnson (2016) notes that potential minority language speaking jurors are often dismissed from juries during the *voir dire* process. In *Hernandez* v. *New York* (1991), the Supreme Court upheld a decision by a New York State Court that a prosecutor may dismiss jurors who are bilingual in Spanish and English from juries with peremptory strikes for fear that they would consider testimony given in Spanish rather than the English interpretation provided by the court interpreter. Johnson (2016) argues that the so-called race neutral peremptory challenge 'creates a generational ban on anyone who speaks Spanish' (Johnson 2016: 960). Likewise, Valentine II (2015) contends that striking prospective multilingual jurors during *voir dire* in a diverse and modern America is unacceptable and unnecessary, citing the 2011 US Court of Appeals for the Fourth Circuit decision in *United States* v. *Cabrera-Beltran* (2011). During the *voir dire* in *Cabrera-Beltran*, three multilingual jurors were dismissed as they refused to disregard any Spanish-language evidence presented at trial and rely exclusively on the English-language interpretation, even if they identified errors in the interpretation (Valentine II 2015). If the US courts' decisions were to be applied to Hong Kong, it would be impossible to empanel a jury, as most jurors nowadays are bilingual in Chinese and English, to varying degrees. The linguistic landscape in the Hong Kong courtroom will be examined in Chapter 4.

This chapter focuses on the linguistic dimensions of juror qualifications. The next section examines the juror language requirements in major common law jurisdictions. It discusses how linguistic diversity arising from an increasingly mobile global population might result in minority language speakers being disadvantaged and discriminated against while exercising their rights and civic duties to serve on juries.

Juror language requirements in Anglo-American common law jurisdictions

This section surveys and compares the relevant laws governing the selection of jurors in major common law jurisdictions including the United Kingdom and former English-speaking British colonies including the United States, Canada, Australia and New Zealand, focusing on juror language requirements. The juror language requirement in Hong Kong together with its linguistic landscape and the operation of the jury system will be examined in detail in Chapter 4.

United Kingdom

In England and Wales, random selection of jurors has been facilitated by computer since 1981 (Lloyd-Bostock & Thomas 1999: 21). Under the Juries Act 1974, all registered parliamentary or local government electors aged between 18 and 76 are eligible for jury service. The Juries Act 1974, however, does not specify a language requirement for jurors, though it does require potential jurors to 'have lived in the United Kingdom, Channel Islands or the Isle of Man for any period of at least five years since they were 13 years old and be eligible to vote in parliamentary or local elections'. The same requirement is also found in Scotland in the Guide to Jury Service Eligibility and Applying for Excusal provided by Scottish Courts and Tribunals Service (Scottish Courts and Tribunals Service n.d.). This is probably based on the presumption that those who have lived in any of the stated areas for at least five years since they were 13 years old must have acquired sufficient English proficiency to understand court proceedings. In Northern Ireland, under the Juries (Northern Ireland) Order 1996, 'persons suffering from mental disorder' and 'persons unable to understand the English language' are ineligible for jury service. Note that people unable to understand English are considered on a par with the mentally disordered in respect of their eligibility for jury service.

Despite the general concerns that black and minority ethnic (BME) groups are underrepresented among summoned jurors, a study conducted by Thomas and Balmer (2007) on the diversity and fairness of the jury system in England and Wales revealed no significant underrepresentation of BME groups among summoned jurors in England and Wales. This might be partly due to the fact that there is no specific English ability requirement for juror eligibility. The abolition of peremptory challenges in England and Wales in 1988 (Law Reform Commission 2010; Lloyd-Bostock & Thomas 1999) might have also contributed to the finding. It can be argued that the abolition of peremptory challenges makes the jury selection process in England and Wales more random and thus arguably more representative than in the United States, where both the jury *voir dire* and the peremptory challenge have been argued to be tools for excluding NES and LEP people from jury service as mentioned above.

Canada

Individual provinces and territories in Canada have their own laws about the eligibility of jurors. In terms of language requirements, in general, one has to speak the language in which the trial is conducted, which can be English or French. For example, Section 4 of the Jury Act of British Columbia (RSBC 1996) states that '[i]f the language in which a trial is to be conducted is one that a person is unable to understand, speak or read, the person is disqualified from serving as a juror in the trial'. In Ontario, under Section 2 (d) of the Juries Act (RSO 1990), only those who 'can speak, read and understand English or French' are eligible and liable to serve as jurors. Hogg (2021: 54) argues that the Canadian justice system is 'a tool of colonial oppression, securing justice for the colonizers at the expense of the colonized'. This, as he suggests, is reflected in the fact that First Nations (Indigenous) people are over-represented in the prison population but significantly underrepresented on juries and among those working in the administration of justice in Ontario. Hogg (2021: 70) argues that it is important to ensure that Indigenous people are adequately represented on juries so as to enhance their confidence in the justice system. Although Hogg (2021: 69) does not raise language barriers as a reason for the under-representation of Indigenous people on juries in Ontario, he suggests that information regarding the jury system should be translated into Indigenous languages before it is distributed to community members. However, he does not go as far as to propose interpreting services for Indigenous people who speak neither English nor French. In a report on First Nations Representation on Ontario Juries, Iacobucci (2013: 5) points out that the requirement for individuals to speak English or French to be eligible for jury service is problematic for First Nations people whose primary language is their Indigenous language. He suggests that First Nations individuals selected to participate on a jury should be offered translation and interpretation services (Iacobucci 2013: 76).

In the Northwest Territories, it is contended that the requirement for jurors to be fluent in English 'effectively excluded most Indigenous persons living in isolated or remote areas where English was not used commonly, if at all' (Davison 2020: 198). However, following an amendment to the Jury Act in 1988, any Canadian citizen having reached the age of 18 and able to speak and understand an official language is qualified to serve as a juror in a trial that may be conducted in English or French in the Northwest Territories and Nunavut (RSNWT [Nu] 1988; see also Leung, 2019: 236). Given that there are 11 official languages in the Northwest Territories, and three in Nunavut, citizens speaking official languages other than English and French cannot sit on juries without the assistance of a court interpreter. Therefore, to effectuate the reforms, the Department of Justice in the Northwest Territories established an interpreter training programme. Interpreters having received the training are deployed to assist the sheriff in assembling jury panels and in providing interpreting services for jurors during the trial (Iacobucci 2013: 41). However, translation and interpretation services for jurors obviously do not cover other non-official languages, including Asian languages, spoken by potential jurors. Given that immigrants account for 23% of the Canadian population as of 2021 (Statistics Canada 2021), there is no knowing how many of these immigrants possess the language ability to participate effectively in court proceedings conducted in a language other than their primary language without the assistance of a court interpreter.

Australia

In Australia, all registered voters aged between 18 and 70 are eligible for jury service, subject to disqualifications and exemptions set out in relevant laws of individual states or territories (Federal Court of Australia Act 1976). An examination of the jury laws across all states and territories indicates that individuals who lack a sufficient understanding of English (Australian Capital Territory Juries Act 1967), cannot read or write in English (Queensland Jury Act 1995), or are unable to adequately communicate in or comprehend the language (Victoria Juries Act 2000) are deemed ineligible for jury service. It is acknowledged that the English language qualification requirement can exclude people from culturally and linguistically diverse backgrounds from jury service, thereby undermining the representativeness of juries (Law Reform Commission of Western Australia 2010: 102). However, it is argued that the necessity for jurors to understand court proceedings is fundamental and should take precedence over the principle of ensuring broad community representation in juries (Law Reform Commission of Western Australia 2010: 102)

Despite the Australian High Court's recognition that the representative jury is central to the integrity of the jury institution, underrepresentation of Indigenous Australians on contemporary juries is a concern in Australia (Hunter & Crittenden 2023). A recent study revealed that while the representation of Aboriginal people and Torres Strait Islanders on juries has improved in recent years, Indigenous Australians are still rarely seen on a jury, even in those parts of Australia with sizeable Indigenous populations (Hunter & Crittenden 2023). The study identified major problems in the law and in its processes that compromise the Indigenous representation on juries. One reason for the exclusion of Aboriginal people from jury participation may be lack of English proficiency (Hunter & Crittenden 2023: 3). The 2014–2015 National Aboriginal and Torres Strait Islander Social Survey indicates that 'around 11% of Aboriginal and Torres Strait Islander people spoke an Australian Indigenous language as their main language at home' (Hunter & Crittenden 2023: 49). In the Northern Territory, over two thirds of Aboriginal people speak an Indigenous language, making it the region with the highest proportion of Indigenous language speakers (Hunter & Crittenden 2023: 49). The practice of peremptory challenges during jury empanelment processes across Australian jurisdictions makes it easier for Aboriginal people to be excluded, often based on concerns about their language ability or other considerations that the challenging party is not required to disclose. It is, however, noted in the study that during jury trials in Australian Capital Territories, non-juror support people are allowed in the jury room at the direction of the judge. Jurors may be given support for performing the jury duties, including 'an interpreter, an Auslan interpreter, an assistance animal, disability aid or support person' (Hunter & Crittenden 2023: 49). The study argues that barriers within the administration of justice impair Indigenous Australians' access to jury service. It suggests that 'all states and territories in Australia explore reasonable support for prospective Indigenous jurors in the jury room and in the courtroom including the provision of interpreters' (Hunter & Crittenden 2023: 49).

As a matter of fact, the English ability requirement impacts not only Indigenous people but also migrant groups, which are likewise underrepresented on juries in Australia (New South Wales Law Reform Commission 2007). According to the New South Wales Law Reform Commission (2007), 95% of people living in Australia are citizens, and 75% of overseas-born Australians are citizens and thus have the right to vote and to serve on juries. It is suggested that the problem of apparent underrepresentation among migrant groups, especially among more recent arrivals, has more to do with the English language requirement and the implementation of peremptory challenge than with them not acquiring an elector's status (New South Wales Law Reform Commission 2007: 28–29).

New Zealand

In New Zealand, Section 6 of the Juries Act 1981 provides that a person who is currently registered as an elector is qualified and liable to serve as a juror (New Zealand Juries Act 1981). Unlike in Australia, where electors have to be Australian citizens, New Zealand allows permanent residents to vote and thus to sit on juries (Cameron et al. 1999). There is no explicit provision in the Juries Act of 1981 that disqualifies individuals based on their inability to understand the English language at a reasonable level (New Zealand Law Commission 2001: 78), although peremptory challenge during jury empanelment is still allowed in New Zealand. It can be argued that by allowing permanent residents to participate in jury service, and by not specifying a language requirement or disqualification, New Zealand juries are more inclusive and representative.

While the existence of a language requirement effectively excludes potential jurors lacking the language proficiency from participating in jury service, thereby undermining the jury representativeness, the absence of such a requirement in New Zealand also presents its own challenges. The system relies on summoned jurors' self-assessment of their English ability or court staff noticing any comprehension difficulties experienced by jurors (New Zealand Law Commission 2001: 78). Upon arrival at court, individuals summoned for jury service are informed, in several languages, that they must be able to speak and understand English; otherwise, they will be excused by the Registrar (Cameron et al. 1999: 121). Nonetheless, a study revealed that eight jurors across seven trials either admitted or were reported by fellow jurors to have encountered difficulties in fully understanding the evidence presented in English, which was their second language (New Zealand Law Commission 2001: 78). As the overseas-born population in New Zealand increased to over a quarter of the total population in 2013, it follows that many people from migrant and refugee backgrounds with limited English proficiency (LEP) have received summons to jury service (Smith 2015: 58). Although summonsed jurors can write to the court to ask for excusal from jury service on the grounds of low English skills, not all may follow this procedure. Even if they do, their requests may not be granted. A significant issue is that the summons information is written in English only, with the exception of the sentence '[i]f you think you may have trouble understanding the trial you should speak to a member of staff at the court', which is translated into Māori and 12 other languages (Smith 2015: 60). Smith's (2015) study revealed that LEP recipients did not understand the summons, and some had to ask their children to translate, while others had to seek help from their language teachers to write letters to the court requesting excusal (Smith 2015).

Smith's (2015) study also indicated that while some summonsed jurors wished to be excused due to concerns about their ability to comprehend the trial, others did not choose to excuse themselves, as they saw participating in jury service as a good opportunity to learn about the democratic nature of the justice system in New Zealand. This was despite their own self-assessment of linguistic inadequacy to be a juror, as they were summonsed for jury service within the first few months of their arrival in New Zealand when they had very limited written and spoken English ability. One migrant whose English was described as 'not perfect' by his English teacher highly valued the opportunity to be included in jury service and regarded his participation as a marker of belonging. It is estimated that 4 in 10 juries of 12 people could contain one juror who cannot hold a conversation in English (Smith 2015: 58). Some problems encountered by jurors from migrant and refugee backgrounds include, among others, 'the speed of spoken language', 'the complexity of sentence structure', 'the density of idiomatic language', 'the use of legal jargon' and 'the wide range of vocabulary needed' (Smith 2015: 62). Smith (2015) questions how court officials and other jurors or judges without proper training could be able to make appropriate assessments of the potential jurors' English proficiency. She argues for specifying English language ability requirements for jury service, as well as for clarifying if interpreting or translation support is available for jurors (Smith 2015: 65). Currently, only sign language interpreters are provided for deaf jurors in New Zealand; the service is not available for LEP jurors (Smith 2015: 63).

As in Canada and Australia, underrepresentation of Indigenous people on juries is a concern in New Zealand. Similarly to First Nations people in Canada, Māori are over-represented as a proportion of defendants in criminal proceedings but underrepresented on juries (New Zealand Law Commission 2001: 68). In addition to English, Māori is an official language in New Zealand under Section 3 of the

Māori Language Act 1987. Section 4 of the Act stipulates the right of all participants in legal proceedings to speak Māori, 'whether or not they are able to understand or communicate in English or any other language' (Māori Language Act 1987). Section 4(3) of the Act provides that '[w]here any person intends to speak Māori in any legal proceedings, the presiding officer shall ensure that a competent interpreter is available'. This section, however, does not apply to jurors (New Zealand Law Commission 2001: 80). The feedback from lawyers to the questionnaires received by the New Zealand Law Commission (2001) does not support the provision of interpreting services for potential jurors who can understand Māori but not English. One of the concerns is that interpreting for a juror from the opening until the verdict of a trial would 'entail considerable expense and delay' in court proceedings. Other concerns are the 'conflict with the principles of direct juror participation in the process of jury discussion and of the secrecy of jury deliberations', noting that there is risk of the interpreter influencing the deliberations. It is thus concluded that persons who cannot understand English should not be permitted to serve on juries (New Zealand Law Commission 2001: 81). Meanwhile, almost all those who speak Māori also understand English, so a Māori juror not understanding English is unlikely to happen in practice (New Zealand Law Commission 2001: 81). This suggests that the underrepresentation of Māori has little to do with the use of English in jury trials in New Zealand. However, while Māori people may not have a problem with proceedings conducted in English and thus do not need interpreting services, other LEP jurors from migrant or refugee backgrounds may need language assistance to fully participate in jury service as discussed above. The issue of interpreting for jurors and the concern of the legal arena about the interpreter as the thirteenth person in the jury room will be discussed in Chapter 7.

United States

In the United States, the language requirements for jury service in the federal courts are mandated by the Jury Selection and Service Act of 1968 ('JSSA'). Section 1865 of the JSSA provides for the qualifications for jury service and states in subsections (b)(2) and (b)(3) that citizens who are 'unable to read, write, and understand the English language with a degree of proficiency sufficient to fill out satisfactorily the juror qualification form' or 'unable to speak the English language' are not qualified for jury service (JSSA 1968). Gonzales Rose (2014) considers the requirement to be a stringent standard as that can exclude anyone who does not speak English very well or lacks written literacy in the English language from the jury pool. Gonzales Rose contends that in communities with high numbers of language minorities, the English language requirement necessarily 'prevents significant numbers of racial and national origin minorities from serving' (Gonzales Rose 2014: 816). Her study estimated the number of LEP citizens in the United States to be 12.8 million, accounting for approximately 9% of the U.S. population (Gonzales Rose 2014: 813–814). Another study revealed that 32 million citizens in the United States do not speak English as their primary language (Johnson 2016: 975). Approximately 44% of Latinos and

40% of Asian Americans have insufficient English proficiency, which suggests a strong relationship between race and English proficiency (Gonzales Rose 2014: 814). It is also noted that over 75% of Latino immigrants in the United States cannot speak English 'very well' (Gonzales Rose 2014: 823).

In Puerto Rico, where Spanish is the dominant language spoken by 95% of adults and 97% of children at home (US Census Bureau 2022), the English language requirement excludes approximately 90% of Puerto Rico's age-eligible population from federal jury service (Gonzales Rose 2011). As Gonzales Rose (2011) observes, black Latinos and other Puerto Ricans of colour, who are more likely to belong to lower socioeconomic classes, tend to have limited English skills, leading to the exclusion of many individuals from such backgrounds from the jury pool. Gonzales Rose (2011) suggests that the exclusion constitutes a violation of defendants' Sixth Amendment right to a jury selected from a fair cross-section of the community. She argues for the provision of interpretation services for NES/LEP jurors to resolve the jury-exclusion dilemma (Gonzales Rose 2011). An examination of the states' juror language requirements revealed that most of the states have similar English language requirements, though the stringency and levels of English proficiency in those requirements vary from state to state (Gonzales 2014; Johnson 2016). Only nine states do not specify any language requirements for juror eligibility (Johnson 2016). However, states which do not have specific English language requirements for jury service must be in the process of instituting such a requirement or using such a requirement in practice (Gonzales Rose 2014: 821), as proficiency in English is a *de facto* requirement whereby NES or LEP individuals appearing in court for jury duty are routinely dismissed by judges (Johnson 2016). As Brown (1994) points out, LEP citizens who fill out the jury qualification form with the assistance of other people are likely to be dismissed from jury service when they are called for jury duty and found to speak no or limited English.

Gonzales Rose (2014) argues that English language requirements can result in juries that are not representative of the community, particularly in areas with significant populations of LEP citizens, like Spanish-speaking Latino communities. This is particularly concerning, as Latinos, like African Americans, are highly overrepresented in the criminal justice system and thus maintaining the diversity of the jury pool is essential in ensuring a fair and just trial for the defendant (Gonzales Rose 2014: 825). The United States has the largest Spanish-speaking population after Mexico (Gonzales Rose 2020). McCann (2017: 355) argues that ensuring that LEP individuals are afforded the same privileges and opportunities as every US citizen is important, especially in the light of the influx of immigrants to the United States. It is argued that jury selection in the United States systematically excludes LEP citizens from jury service and that the English-language requirement 'serves as a discriminatory instrument of exclusion' (Johnson 2016: 984). The exclusion of NES or LEP citizens from the jury pool is argued to be language and racial discrimination, as well as a violation of the defendant's right to a trial by an impartial jury drawn from a fair cross-section of the community (e.g. Brown 1994; Chávez 2008; Duffy 2017; Gonzales Rose 2014, 2020; Johnson 2016; McCann 2017; Ramirez 1994).

Gonzales Rose (2014: 831) contends that '[j]uror language requirements simultaneously infringe upon a criminal defendant's right to a fair trial and LEP citizens' right to participate in self-governance vis-à-vis a jury panel'.

The only state in the United States that allows NES and LEP citizens to sit on juries is New Mexico. Under the Constitution of New Mexico, all citizens have the right to serve on juries whether or not they are able to speak, read or write English or Spanish. Certified court interpreters are used to assist jurors in need of the service (Chávez 2008; Duffy 2017; Gonzales Rose 2014, 2020; Johnson 2016; Kisor 2001; Leung 2019). It is argued that New Mexico should serve as a model for all the other states in the United States to include NES and LEP citizens in juries with the assistance of certified court interpreters (Chávez 2008; Duffy 2017; Gonzales Rose 2014, 2020; Johnson 2016; Kisor 2001). This will be discussed in more detail in Chapter 7.

Language requirements and jury comprehension

Trial by jury has a long history in the common law legal system and is seen as both a symbol of democracy and a practical way of enhancing social coherence. A randomly selected jury which is representative of the community is generally regarded as an essential characteristic of the jury institution. While it is important to ensure that jurors selected to sit on trials have a sufficient command of the language in which the trial is conducted, the language requirement necessarily excludes those who lack the language proficiency but would otherwise qualify for jury service. This is concerning in communities with a significant NES or LEP population and goes against the notion of trial by peers. Creating barriers to random selection and equal participation can compromise the representativeness of juries. The ability to understand and/or speak English has always been a criterion for the jurors in the jurisdictions examined above, and all have significant numbers of NES and LEP people whose primary language is not English. Since most NES or LEP persons are either Indigenous people or migrant ethnic minorities, it is argued that the systematic exclusion of NES and LEP persons from the jury pool is both linguistic and racial discrimination (Brown 1994; Duffy 2017; Gonzales Rose 2014, 2020; Johnson 2016; Kisor 2001).

On the other hand, requiring jurors to understand the language used in court is necessary to ensure that their decision is an informed one. This highlights the tensions between maintaining random selection of jurors and ensuring that the jurors possess a sufficient proficiency in the court language in order to understand the court proceedings. As a matter of fact, jury comprehension is a problem faced not only by NES or LEP persons but is encountered even by jurors who speak English as their primary language. Studies on jury comprehension reveal that jurors often struggle to understand jury instructions, which typically contain legal jargon that is difficult for ordinary citizens to comprehend. The next chapter will explore the issue of jury comprehension in Anglo-American courtrooms and discuss how jury comprehension problems might compromise the delivery of justice or the defendant's right to a fair trial.

Note

1. I had the privilege of observing the jury *voir dire* of a civil trial held in the Suffolk County Superior Court in Boston (*Kinnally* v. *R.J. Reynolds, et al.* [2023] 1684CV03937) on 5 January 2023 during my one-year fellowship at Harvard University as a visiting scholar. It was a lawsuit against a tobacco company litigated by the husband of a woman who died of lung cancer after having smoked for over 50 years. During the jury *voir dire*, the prospective jurors were asked by both parties about issues including their history of smoking, their attitude towards smoking, and if they had any family members or friends who had smoked and died of lung cancer. In the end, only those who were considered to be neutral in their attitude towards smoking and had no friends or family members who had smoked and died of lung cancer were selected to sit on the jury.

3

Jury Comprehension in Anglo-American Courtrooms

The previous chapter delved into the institution of trial by jury, reviewed juror language requirements in Anglo-American jurisdictions, and discussed how language requirements for potential jurors might create barriers to equal participation while violating the principle of random selection and trial by one's peers. The chapter highlighted the tensions between maintaining the fundamental principle of trial by jury and the need to ensure those selected to sit on juries possess a sufficient command of the English language to comprehend court proceedings. This chapter explores how legal discourse in court proceedings can pose comprehension problems even for jurors who meet the language requirement to serve on trials. It examines concerns about jurors' ability to understand legal discourse (in particular, jury instructions often delivered in inaccessible language), discusses how the nature of legal English might impact jurors' comprehension, and reviews relevant literature and illustrative anecdotal evidence. This chapter also discusses the concept of judges' audiences when delivering jury instructions in an attempt to account for their reluctance to deviate from standard jury instructions. Finally, it examines the Voice Projection Framework proposed by Heffer (2018) for analysing the (mis)communications between the trial judge and the jury in a high-profile English case, as well as exploring its applicability to the study presented in this book.

Concerns about jurors' ability to understand jury instructions

Legal language, specifically legal English for the purpose of this book, is notoriously difficult for laypersons to understand and has faced criticism for being overly complex and pretentious, as noted in Chapter 1. Trial by jury uses laypersons drawn from the community as fact-finders in the judicial process, and these individuals generally lack familiarity with the law and legal language. They are required to decide the outcome of a trial after hearing all the evidence, legal arguments and instructions about the case. This gives rise to concerns about jurors' ability to comprehend courtroom discourse, especially jury instructions, which are typically written in dense legalistic language and presented orally (Tiersma 1999: 231). Dumas (2000: 51) observes that jury instructions are often 'modelled upon the language of appellate opinions' written by judges for their fellow judges to read, not intended be read aloud to the addressee. Orally presenting a text written in dense and complex language intended to be read adds to the difficulty in processing the message. The United States Supreme Court Justice Felix Frankfurter once said that a judge's instructions to jurors were 'abracadabra' (Tiersma 1999: 231), while the Appeal Court in *Structural Rubber Products* v. *Park Rubber* (1984) suggested that the language used in jury instructions are often so archaic and unrealistic that even in simple cases what the jurors hear is 'little more than legal mumbo jumbo to them'. This has long been the case; as Frank (1930: 195) noted almost a century ago, the judge's instructions to the jury 'might as well be in a foreign language – that, indeed, for all the jury's understanding of them, they are spoken in a foreign language'. What, then, makes legal language or jury instructions so difficult to understand? This will be discussed in the next section.

Language of the law

First of all, the convoluted nature of legal language is associated with the origins and development of the legal language in England. The origins of legal English can be traced back to ancient Britain, where it evolved through the influence of various waves of invasions (Mellinkoff 1963; Tiersma 1999, 2008). The language of the law has been shaped by various communities, including Celtic-speaking Britons, Anglo-Saxon mercenaries, Scandinavian raiders, Latin-speaking clerics, Norman invaders and lawyers themselves (Tiersma 1999: 2). Consequently, legal language has preserved numerous terms from Anglo-Saxon (Old English), Latin and French origins (Mellinkoff 1963; Tiersma 1999). Celtic, which was the dominant language of Britain until the Roman occupation (Mellinkoff 1963: 37), however, has had little lasting impact on legal English (Tiersma 1999: 9). Although the Anglo-Saxons did not seem to have developed a distinct legal profession, there is evidence that they did have a form of legal language. Some remnants of the Anglo-Saxon legal language which have survived to this day include 'guilt', 'manslaughter' and 'murder' (Tiersma 1999: 9). Throughout a significant portion of its history, the English legal profession practised a form of trilingualism, utilising English, French and Latin in different contexts, with lawyers frequently engaging in codeswitching (Tiersma 1999: 33). Due to the relics from Old English, French and Latin, legal English can be quite different from ordinary speech and writing to the extent that some have argued that lawyers speak a separate language (Tiersma 1999: 3). Some even contend that legal jargon is used to deliberately 'befuddle the public' (Tiersma 1999: 87).

The following are some characteristics of legal English as identified by Mellinkoff (1963):

1. Frequent use of common words with uncommon meanings (e.g. 'action' for 'lawsuit' and 'save' for 'except')

2. Frequent use of Old English and Middle English words not commonly used in everyday English now (e.g. 'aforesaid' and 'forthwith')
3. Frequent use of Latin words and phrases (e.g. '*mens rea*' and 'quasi')
4. Use of Old French and Anglo-Norman words (e.g. 'heir' and 'tort')
5. Use of terms of art (e.g. 'fee simple' and 'habeas corpus') and argot ('purported' and 'without prejudice')
6. Frequent use of formal words ('prior' instead of 'before' and 'subsequent' instead of 'after').

Mellinkoff's description of the characteristics of legal English is largely echoed by Tiersma (1999), who suggests that in addition to the use of archaic, formal and unusual words, legal English also favours the use of impersonal constructions, nominalisations, passives, modal verbs (as in the use of 'shall' to mean 'must') and multiple negations, as well as long and complex sentences and poor organisation. All these factors contribute to the inaccessibility of legal English to laypersons.

Studies in jury comprehension and methods

Studies in jury comprehension have primarily been contextualised in Anglo-American courtrooms, particularly in the United States. In the United Kingdom, it has been suggested that the existence of the Contempt of Court Act 1981 tends to inhibit jury research in English Crown Courts (Heffer 2005: 159). This is because Section 8 of the Contempt of Court Act 1981 makes it an offence to 'obtain, disclose or solicit any particulars of statements made, opinions expressed, arguments advanced, or votes cast by members of a jury in the course of their deliberations' (Contempt of Court Act 1981). Thomas (2008, 2010), however, contends that Section 8 does not actually prevent most research about juries, though she agrees that the existence of the Act has created confusion about the types of research that can be conducted with jurors (Thomas 2008: 8; 2010: 1). This might have contributed to the dearth of jury research in the United Kingdom and in other common law jurisdictions, including Hong Kong.

Jury studies have largely focused on the comprehensibility of jury instructions, which are provided by judges to inform jurors about trial procedures and to direct them on the law as it applies to the case at trial. These instructions are referred to as specimen directions in the United Kingdom and in Hong Kong, while in the United States, they are known as pattern jury instructions (Gibbons 2017). As mentioned earlier, standard jury instructions are often written in legalese, making them difficult for laypersons to understand. Previous research has highlighted concerns that misunderstandings or lack of comprehension can lead to miscarriages of justice. In capital cases, jurors' comprehension or otherwise incomprehension of the judge's guidance can literally be a matter of life and death (Tiersma 1999: 233). Unlike judges in bench trials, jurors are not required to explain or justify their verdicts, which makes it challenging to detect or address any misunderstandings of the judge's instructions. Therefore, research into jury comprehension is crucial for understanding this significant issue.

Two mainstream methods have been employed by researchers to assess jurors' comprehension of legal directions. The first method is to assess jurors' objective comprehension, while the other relies on jurors' subjective self-report of their comprehension of judicial instructions (McKimmie et al. 2014). A pioneering study in jury comprehension by Charrow and Charrow (1979) adopted an objective paraphrase approach to assess the comprehensibility of civil jury instructions in California. By asking jurors to paraphrase the meaning of speech segments of pre-recorded jury instructions, the study identified specific linguistic features typical of legalese that hinder comprehension. Many of these features were previously noted by Mellinkoff (1963) and Tiersma (1999). The problematic linguistic elements identified by Charrow and Charrow (1979) include, among others, 'overuse of nominalisations', the use of 'as to' in lieu of 'about', 'misplaced phrases', 'whiz (that is, which is) and completement deletion', 'use of double or triple negatives', 'poor discourse structures' and 'too many embeddings'. The study indicated that the mean percentage of correct paraphrasing of speech segments containing such linguistic features ranged from 24% to 28.6%. For legal terminology such as 'credibility' and 'proximate cause', the mean correct paraphrasing was 32%, while the more common term 'discrepancy' or its plural form 'discrepancies' was correctly paraphrased 89% of the time. Truncated passives and passives used in subordinate clauses were also found to be more poorly understood than full passives and passives used in main clauses (Charrow & Charrow 1979). The study revealed that rewriting the instructions in plain English and eliminating the problematic linguistic features as far as possible significantly improved the subjects' understanding of the instructions.

A later study by Steele and Thornburg (1991) using a similar paraphrase approach and pre-recorded jury instructions corroborated the findings of Charrow and Charrow's (1979) study, but revealed even lower comprehension rates. In their study, subjects who had been summoned for jury service in Dallas County, Texas, but had never served on a jury, were asked to paraphrase five legal terms from Texas jury instructions: 'proximate cause', 'new and independent cause', 'negligence', 'presumption of innocence' and 'accomplice testimony'. The study found that the instructions were largely incomprehensible to the prospective jurors, as their correct paraphrasing percentages were extremely low. For example, the subjects correctly paraphrased only 5.83% of the pattern instruction on 'new and independent cause', and the corresponding figures for 'accomplice testimony', 'negligence', 'proximate cause' and 'presumption of innocence' were 9.3%, 19.49%, 14.55% and 17.37%, respectively. Similar to Charrow and Charrow's (1979) findings, Steele and Thornburg's (1991) study demonstrated that rewritten instructions with improved syntactic structures and more comprehensible vocabulary were much better understood with significantly higher correct paraphrasing percentages.

The second commonly employed method uses a subjective self-report approach whereby jurors are asked to rate their comprehension levels of legal instructions. These studies tend to yield higher comprehension rates, which is apparently at odds with the findings of research using an objective approach (McKimmie et al. 2014). For example, a study conducted by Trimboli (2008) in New South Wales, Australia, used a questionnaire to obtain information on jurors' comprehension of judicial instructions and other aspects of the criminal trial process. The results revealed that close to 95% of the jurors stated that they either 'completely understood' the judge's instructions on the law or 'understood most things the judge said'. In evaluating the study, the researcher emphasised that the study relied on jurors' self-reported understanding of the judge's instructions, and that jurors 'may not have been entirely candid in their responses about their levels of comprehension or they may believe that they understood when perhaps they did not' (Trimboli 2008: 11).

Given the divergent results generated by the two different methods, McKimmie et al.'s (2014) study adopted a dual approach by measuring jurors' subjective and objective comprehensions of judicial instructions. Jurors in the Supreme and District courts in Brisbane, Australia were invited to fill out a survey within two months of the trials to reflect on their comprehension of two legal terms, 'beyond reasonable doubt' and 'burden of proof'. They first asked jurors to rate their understanding of the terms 'burden of proof' and 'beyond reasonable doubt' before asking them to explain the two in their own words. A majority of the jurors reported that they understood both terms very well. On a 7-point scale with 1 and 7 on each end representing 'not at all' and 'very much', respectively, the comprehension means for both terms were 5.97 (85%) and 6.64 (95%), respectively. The objective paraphrase test, however, revealed that a substantial proportion of the jurors were actually mistaken about the meanings of both terms.

A study conducted in Winchester in the United Kingdom by Thomas (2010) using case simulation revealed a similar trend. The study aimed to find out, among other things, jurors' perception of their ability to understand the judge's legal instructions and their actual comprehension of the judge's instructions. Findings of the study showed that 68% of the jurors taking part in the simulated case indicated that the judge's instructions were easy to understand. However, when asked to identify the two questions in which they were explicitly directed by the judge to determine whether or not the defendant had acted in self-defence, only 31% of the jurors were able to accurately identify the two questions. These findings seem to suggest that the subjective method, which relies on jurors' self-reported understanding of judicial instructions, may not be entirely reliable.

Anecdotal reports about jury comprehension problems

Jury comprehension problems are occasionally reflected in anecdotal reports regarding juries' lack of understanding of legal instructions. In the 2007 manslaughter conviction of Keran Henderson, dissenting jurors claimed after the verdict that the majority of the jury did not fully comprehend the evidence (Thomas 2010: 5). The jury foreman was interviewed by *The Times* newspaper, and the interview was published by the newspaper, resulting in both parties being found guilty of contempt by the High Court (ibid.: 5), obviously under Section 8 of the Contempt of Court Act 1981 mentioned earlier.

Jury comprehension issues can also manifest when juries communicate with judges through notes during deliberations (Dumas 2000; Heffer 2018; Steele & Thornburg 1991). However, in most cases, when jurors express confusion, judges tend to simply reread the original instructions instead of rephrasing them in language that is more easily understood by lay jurors, as if it were a matter of not hearing rather than not understanding. Unfortunately, rereading the instructions contributes little to the jurors' comprehension (Dumas 2000; Heffer 2018). Dumas (2000) cited the US case of *Weeks* v. *Angelone* (2000), in which the jury directed a question to the judge regarding the sentencing options, namely life imprisonment or the death penalty. The judge, having discussed the matter with defence counsel, decided that he could not provide a clearer answer to the jurors' question. Instead, he simply directed their attention to the relevant section of the jury instructions. The defendant was subsequently sentenced to death by the jury. This does not appear to be an isolated incident, as Steele and Thornburg's (1991) study cited more cases in the United States demonstrating jurors' confusion about legal instructions and the courts' reluctance to correct the confusion.

Another example of an attempt by the jury to obtain clarification is the English case of *Regina* v. *Christopher Huhne and Vasiliki Pryce* (*R.* v. *Pryce* 2013), cited and examined in some detail by Heffer (2018). In *R.* v. *Pryce* (2013), the defendant, Vasiliki Pryce, was tried in London for perverting the course of justice by taking driving penalty points for her then husband. She claimed that she had been driving at the time of the speeding offence which had been committed by her husband. Her husband eventually pleaded guilty, but Pryce asserted her innocence and based her defence on marital coercion, alleging that she was forced by her husband to take the penalty points for him. During deliberations, the jury sent ten questions to the judge, asking him to clarify his legal directions and the constraints on their deliberations. The judge concluded that those questions indicated fundamental deficits in the jurors' understanding. Nonetheless, instead of answering those questions to clear up the jurors' confusion, the judge reiterated the instructions in his responses to their questions, emphasising that the answers could be found in his oral instructions and the written copies provided to the jury. The case was widely reported in the media, which dubbed the jury a 'dumb' jury, and the competence of the jury was called into question. Heffer (2018), however, argues that the questions raised are mostly reasonable questions and are not indicative of a dumb jury. On the contrary, Heffer (2018) opines that several of the jury's questions demonstrated the jurors' legal-linguistic competence and that they were perceptive about indeterminacies in the judge's directions.

One of the questions asked by the jury in *R.* v. *Pryce* (2013) is 'Can you define what is reasonable doubt?', and the following is the judge's response (Heffer 2018: 225):

> The prosecution must make you feel sure beyond reasonable doubt. A reasonable doubt is a doubt that is reasonable. These are ordinary English words that the law does not allow me to help you with, beyond the written directions.

As revealed in the studies cited earlier in this chapter, 'reasonable doubt' is a term of art and a legal concept which many jurors struggle to comprehend. The following section attempts to explore the reasons why judges are reluctant to depart from standardised jury instructions and to explain legal concepts in simple and easily understood language. The Voice Project Framework used by Heffer for his analysis of the miscommunication between the judge and the jury in this case is examined in the latter part of this chapter.

Judges' audiences in jury instructions

It has been suggested that the reluctance of judges to depart from standard instructions stems from their consciousness of not only their primary audience (that is, the jury) but also their secondary audience, that is, the appellate courts. In the event of an appeal, appellate courts have to review the trial judge's legal directions to decide whether or not the jury has been properly instructed (Dumas 2000; Heffer 2005, 2018; Gibbons 2017). As a matter of fact, appellate courts are not merely a secondary audience for pattern instructions; they may also be the authors of them through prior court decisions that made explicit what appeal courts want the instructions to cover. It is also suggested that pattern jury instructions were developed to 'minimize the use of jury instructions as a tool to obtain appellate reversal' (Kramer & Koenig 1990: 404). Therefore, in instructing the jury, one of the subsidiary goals of the judge is to avoid appellate reversal (Dumas 2000: 51; Gibbons 2017: 144), and appellate courts tend to focus on the legal aspect of the instructions rather than on the comprehensibility of those instructions to jurors (Gibbons 2017: 144). This secondary purpose of avoiding appellate reversals has been found to dominate the primary goal of informing the jury, thereby undermining jurors' comprehension. Heffer (2018) suggests that when instructing juries, judges have at least three audiences in mind: the jury, lawyers for both parties and the appellate court judges, and in high-profile cases, the media can be another audience that judges are mindful of. The 'two audience dilemma' (Gibbons 2017: 143) or the judge's awareness of multiple audiences (Heffer 2005, 2018) are therefore likely to compromise jurors' comprehension.

The audience types proposed by Bell (1984) under his audience and referee design framework can be used to explain judges' audiences in jury instructions and to account for the style-shifting. Bell (1984) proposes four audience types: addressees (listeners who are known, ratified and addressed), auditors (listeners who are not directly addressed but are known and ratified), overhearers (non-ratified listeners of whom the speaker is aware) and eavesdroppers (non-ratified listeners of whom the speaker is unaware).

When instructing the jury, the judge's addressees must be members of the jury, who are directly addressed, known and ratified. The legal parties are auditors, who are not directly addressed, but their presence is authorised (ratified) and known to the speaker. Since judges instructing the jury are mindful of appellate courts (and the media in high-profile cases), the appellate courts (and the media) fall into the audience role as the overhearers, whom judges are aware of although they are not ratified participants in the communication process. According to Bell (1984: 145), speakers adjust their language style primarily to their addressees, and auditors and overhearers as third persons affect speakers' language style 'to a lesser but regular degree'. Since eavesdroppers are not known to the speaker, they are not expected to have an impact on the speaker's language style. In jury instructions, however, it has been observed that judges do not often take jurors' comprehension as their primary concern and adjust their language style accordingly. Instead, they tend to accommodate more to appellate courts as overhearers and third persons, who are not physically present in the courtroom as the speech is delivered. This style shift is called referee design, which happens when a speaker diverges from the addressee towards a third party not physically present in an interaction (Bell 1984: 186). According to Bell (1984: 186; see also Bell 2002: 147), 'referees are third persons not physically present at an interaction, but possessing such salience for a speaker that they influence speech even in their absence'. Referee design is also referred to as initiative style shifts as speakers shift their style 'to identify more strongly with their own ingroup, or to an outgroup with which they wish to identify' (Bell 2002: 147). As noted earlier, the reason why judges are reluctant to depart from standard jury instructions is that the wording of the instructions might have come from prior appellate opinions. In case the outcome of a jury trial is challenged and ends up as a judicial appeal, the first thing an appellate court will do is review the trial judge's instructions to see if the jury has been properly instructed. Adhering to standard instructions avoids appellate reversals, and the comprehensibility of the jury instructions is not the trial judge's primary concern. Thus, appellate courts as absent referees do possess a powerful influence and impact the language style of the trial judge, who is arguably speaking to the absent referees rather than the present addressees. It can also be seen as a manifestation of the judge's in-group identification with their fellow legal professionals, including lawyers in court and the absent appellate court judges.

The operation of the jury system is based on the presumption that jurors understand and follow legal instructions (Ritter 2004). Research into jurors' ability to understand legalistic jury instructions has, however, demonstrated otherwise. The following sections explore other attributes in courtroom communication that might also contribute to jury comprehension problems.

Courtroom communication: Unequal footings for participants

The courtroom is a 'highly role- and rule-governed environment' (Cotterill 2003: 92). The participant roles (legal professionals versus witnesses and jurors as lay participants) and the rules and procedures of the trial process dictate who has the right to speak and what they can say. For example, witnesses are expected to answer, not ask, questions. If a witness fails to confirm or negate a suggestion or declarative question from counsel by responding with a lengthy reply, they will be instructed to restrict their answer to a 'yes' or a 'no'.

In jury trials, the discourse imbalance between judges as experts on law and jurors as experts on facts is another under-researched factor that may present comprehension challenges for jurors (Dumas 2000). Dumas (2000) observes that judges are accorded a much higher level of respect than jurors, as judges are free to enter and leave the courtroom, speak and make rules during a trial. On the other hand, jurors are not supposed to speak but only to listen most of the time and 'are often confined almost as much as prisoners are' (Dumas 2000: 55). The analogy of jurors as prisoners may sound a little exaggerated, but the procedural constraints in court do limit jurors' right to speak. Be it a monologic interaction such as jury instructions or counsel addresses, in which jurors are direct addressees, or a dialogic communication as in witness examination, jurors sit in the jury box as silent listeners throughout. The only jury member with a speaker role is the jury foreperson, who is tasked with telling the court the verdict at the end of the trial. However, in California courtrooms, unlike courts in England and Wales, the verdict is not even delivered by the jury foreperson but by the court clerk (Cotterill 2003: 118). The jury foreperson acts only as the spokesperson for the other members of the jury. Any requests or clarifications about the evidence or legal speeches presented in court must be communicated to the court via the jury foreperson. This necessarily means that, unlike interlocutors in other communication settings, jurors cannot seek clarification at will from the speaker or raise a comprehension problem spontaneously as the speech or evidence is presented in the courtroom.

Voice Projection Framework as a model of legal-lay communication

As demonstrated and discussed above, studies have focused on the convoluted nature of legal language in terms of its terminology, syntax and discursive structure and examined its impact on jurors' comprehension of jury instructions encoded in typical legal language. Research has, however, largely ignored another important facet in jury comprehension, that is, the manner in which these instructions are delivered (Dumas 2000). One major reason for the exclusion of this topic in jury comprehension research is that studies across the board have been based on textual analyses, with a focus on the legalistic features of the language used rather than on naturally occurring data such as audio recording of courtroom proceedings. Even in Charrow and Charrow's (1979) and in Steel and Thornburg's (1991) studies in which audio-recorded speech segments were used, the recordings were prepared by the researchers rather than extracted from authentic recorded court proceedings. The researchers' focus was on identifying legalese and comparing comprehension levels when the legalese identified was eliminated and rephrased in plain English. Later studies, including those mentioned above, have focused on the language used by judges in their oral presentation of legal instructions, and few have delved into the manner in which the instructions are delivered and how this might impact the jurors' comprehension. As we know, in oral presentation, the delivery of a message plays a crucial role in ensuring effective comprehension by the listeners. A poorly delivered speech may result in confusion, misinterpretation and disengagement. In jury instructions, as observed by Dumas (2000: 66), '[n]othing could be worse, from a communication science perspective, than having these instructions read verbatim by a berobed judge to captive jurors in an official monotone. Unfortunately, that is the way the instructions are often communicated'. This important aspect of communication has been hitherto largely overlooked by researchers.

The Voice Projection Framework proposed by Heffer (2018) approaches the jury comprehension issue from both the style of the language used in the instructions and the manner in which those instructions are delivered. Heffer (2018) uses the Voice Projection Framework to explain the fundamental deficit in understanding or miscommunication between the judge and the jury, taking the aforementioned case of *R.* v. *Pryce* (2013) as a model.

According to Heffer (2018), voice comprises three key elements: perspective, projection and responsive understanding. Perspective is the message the speaker wishes to project to a listener or an audience; projection is the way voice carries to an audience; and responsive understanding is the minimal level of response the speaker aims to receive from a listener or audience when conveying their perspective (Heffer 2018: 211–212). When voices fail to carry, miscommunication or fundamental deficits in understanding will result, which may lead to ignoring, miscued affect or plain misunderstanding. Voicing and hearing are the communication aspects of projection. Voicing involves both physical and discursive projection of the speaker's perspective to the audience. Physical voicing is the animating of the speaker's voice 'through sound, sign and other forms of semiosis' (ibid.: 212). In institutional contexts, when the performative elements of animation are conveyed through indirect discourse or written form, it can result in the loss of both physical voice and meaning, as all the expressive and emotional qualities that are inherent in direct speech are lost (ibid.: 212).

Discursive voicing, or styling, refers to 'the selecting and arranging of words, sentences, paragraphs and so on' for projecting voice, which involves the speaker's strategic choices between conforming by following standards and creating to show individuality (ibid.: 212).

Hearing encompasses both the physical act of listening or reading and the cognitive process of comprehension. The projection of voice can falter when the audience is not attentive, has impaired hearing or reading abilities, or when the discourse is overly intricate and the hearer/reader lacks sufficient intelligence to grasp it (ibid.: 212). According to Heffer (2018), projection concerns not only the way a message is voiced and heard but also the extent to which speakers and hearers commit to authority and/or accommodation. Authority refers to the source of institutional power which constrains a speaker's voice projection by imposing discursive and other norms through the process of centring and authorising (ibid.: 214). Conversely, accommodation refers to the degree to which speakers adapt their speech style to the audience by means of converging and persuading (ibid.: 214). Heffer (2018: 215) suggests that for a voice to be successfully projected to the audience, it is important for the speaker to orient towards persuading rather than to simply inform the audience. When judges are merely animating or reciting authoritative legal texts without accommodating to jurors as a lay audience, their voices fail to carry or to result in responsive understanding of the jurors. This, according to Heffer (2018), was the case in *R.* v. *Pryce* (2013).

In *R.* v. *Pryce* (2013), the judge's legal directions on marital coercion combined both a recitation of authoritative legal discourse and the judge's own words stylistically confirming to legal register with the use of long and complex sentences and legal terminology. Heffer (2018: 220) contends that such legal directions 'will not project well to a jury unversed in such language'. Heffer (2018) also notes that jurors come from all walks of life and are put together to form a jury based on the concept of locality. He observes that the locality of Southwark, where the *R* v. *Pryce* (2013) trial was held, is 'particularly heterogeneous', with 34% and 32% of its population born outside the United Kingdom and belonging to ethnic minorities, respectively (Heffer 2018: 215). This suggests that their ability to understand the legal instructions was likely to differ, and jurors born outside the country and/or belonging to ethnic minorities might not have had a sufficient command of the English language to fully understand the proceedings, let alone the intricacies of legal English.

It is important to note that Heffer's (2018) analysis of the judge's directions was entirely based on textual records. He was therefore not able to comment on the judge's physical voicing, such as whether those legal instructions were delivered in a monotone voice, at a rapid pace, or without appropriate pauses, stress or other suprasegmental features that enhance rhetorical effectiveness. This limitation leaves unanswered questions about how such factors might impact the jurors' comprehension in this context.

As regards the voice or voicing of the jurors in their presentation of the ten questions to the judge, Heffer (2018) observes that, discursively, the questions posed by the jury exhibited a notable degree of competence in legal communication and a deliberate effort to converge with legal discourse. However, he contends that since jurors are literally dumb in the sense that they are speechless during the entire trial, what Dumas (2000) refers to as discourse imbalance, they had to submit the questions collectively in written form. This means that the distinctive physical voices of individual jurors, including their physical, discursive and rhetorical characteristics, are lost (Heffer 2018: 216).

Research gaps in jury comprehension

As demonstrated above, jury comprehension is a substantive issue, given its significance in the administration of justice. As Tiersma (2009) observes, a defendant's right to a trial by their peers has little meaning if these peers do not understand the law and the evidence that governs their decisions. Research to date has largely presented the jury comprehension issue as a legal-lay communication problem, arising primarily from the convoluted nature of legal language and judges' reluctance to deviate from standard legal instructions.

Research has yet to explore other contexts where jury comprehension is not merely an intralingual communication issue between legal professionals and laypeople but also an interlingual and intercultural communication problem. Besides, as noted by Dumas (2000), research has largely ignored a vital facet in jury comprehension: the manner in which legal instructions are delivered, that is, physical voicing in

Heffer's (2018) terminology, and its impact on jurors' comprehension. The dearth of studies on this is related to the text-based methodologies adopted across the board, understandably arising from the difficulty of accessing audio recordings of court proceedings for research purposes. The use of authentic audio recordings of court proceedings in the study presented in this book has made it possible to apply Heffer's (2018) Voice Projection Framework to examine not only the impact of speakers' discursive voicing but also that of their physical voicing on jury comprehension. This book aims to address these aspects in the following chapters.

4

The Hong Kong Juries and Courts

As mentioned in the previous chapter, research on jury comprehension has predominantly focused on Anglo-American courtrooms and explored how the use of legal language might create challenges for laypersons unfamiliar with the legal discourse and register. However, there has been little research into jurors' ability to understand courtroom discourse delivered in a language which they speak only as an L2 and how this linguistic disadvantage might further impede their ability to understand courtroom discourse. This chapter presents such a linguistic landscape in which the jury system operates, specifically within the Hong Kong courtroom. In Hong Kong, English trials are now frequently conducted with juries primarily composed of individuals who have English as their L2. This is due to the fact that the local population mostly speaks Cantonese, while English continues to hold an official status as a colonial heritage language. This chapter provides an overview of the operation of the jury system and the practice of court interpreting, which has long been an indispensable service to the courts of Hong Kong. It reviews anecdotal and empirical evidence illustrating comprehension challenges faced by Chinese jurors sitting on English-medium trials.

Elite colonial juries

The jury system was imported to Hong Kong from England in 1845 by the Ordinance for the Regulation of Jurors and Juries, following the British colonisation of Hong Kong in 1843 (Duff et al. 1990, 1992). The 1845 Ordinance (No. 7 §1) stipulated that the jury in Hong Kong should comprise six members, instead of twelve, due to the difficulties in mustering from the small population citizens who were fit and qualified to act as jurors (Duff et al. 1990, 1992; Law Reform Commission of Hong Kong 2010). The size of the jury was subsequently increased to seven by virtue of Ordinance 11 of 1864, Section 2; in 1986, the Jury (Amendment) Ordinance was enacted to empower a judge to increase the number of jurors to nine if appropriate

(Duff et al. 1990, 1992; Law Reform Commission of Hong Kong 2010). The amendment was instigated because of a complicated fraud case,[1] as it was anticipated that some jurors might have to be excused during the course of the long trial for one reason or another (Duff et al. 1990, 1992; Law Reform Commission of Hong Kong 2010). Unlike in the United States, where jury verdicts have to be unanimous, in Hong Kong, a majority of 5 to 2 or 6 to 1 in a seven-member jury panel is accepted by the court as a majority verdict; in a nine-member panel, a majority verdict is either 8 to 1 or 7 to 2; if the number of jurors has been reduced to five either in a seven- or nine-member panel due to the death or discharge of jurors, the verdict must be unanimous (Jury Ordinance, § 24[3] 1999).

In Hong Kong, jury trials have long been reserved only for the more serious criminal cases tried in the High Court, and can also be used in some civil cases such as defamation and malicious prosecution. Death inquests in the Coroner's Court can be held with or without a jury; where a person dies while in official custody, the inquest must be held with a jury, and a jury in the Coroner's Court comprises five members (Judiciary 2020). In the Coroner's Court, a verdict requires only a simple majority of the jurors (Coroners Ordinance, § 42 [1] 1998).

As mentioned earlier in this book, one fundamental principle that underpins the operation of the jury system is that a jury is presumed to represent a randomly selected cross-section of the populace. This, however, has not been the case in Hong Kong. The Hong Kong jury was dubbed 'an oddity' (Duff et al. 1990: 881) or 'a unique and peculiar institution' (Duff et al. 1992: 51) due to its lack of representativeness of the community at large, especially in the early colonial days. The unrepresentativeness of the Hong Kong jury is primarily a result of the requirement for jurors to be proficient in English, which has been an official language in Hong Kong since the commencement of British colonial rule in the territory in 1842. It was not until 1974 that Chinese was accorded the status as an additional official language in Hong Kong. This subsequently led to the lifting of the English-only restriction at different court levels in stages from 1974 to 1997, first in the Magistrates' Courts, then in the District Court and finally in the High Court (see Ng 2018: 205). In the Court of Final Appeal, English is the default language to this day due to the ongoing presence of expatriate non-Chinese-speaking judges or counsel. Despite the increasing use of Chinese in the Magistrates' Courts and the District Courts over the past decades since the 1997 sovereignty handover, the majority of criminal trials are still heard in English before a judge and a jury in the High Court. In 2023, only 21.1% of the criminal trials in the High Court were held in Chinese (Department of Justice 2023).

The jury pool, known locally as the List of Common Jurors (formerly the Jury List and then the Jurors List) is compiled by the Registrar of the High Court (formerly the Supreme Court) based on information furnished by the Commissioner of the Immigration Department. In the early colonial days, the jury pool consisted only of English-speaking expatriates because people ignorant of the English language were automatically disqualified (Duff et al. 1990, 1992). As a result, this jury pool represented only a tiny percentage of the total population. For instance, there were only 119 jurors on the 1854 List (Hong Kong Government 1854), accounting for only 0.2% of the total population of around 60,000 people (Munn 2001), and tellingly, all the jurors had European names (Hong Kong Government 1854). In 1858, the first Chinese name Wong A Shing (also known as Wong Shing) appeared on the List (Pomerantz-Zhang 2012; Smith & Munn 2005; see also Hong Kong Government 1858). He was one of the first three Chinese students sent to the United States in 1847 for studies at Yale University, and the second Chinese to serve in the Legislative Council (Pomerantz-Zhang 2012; Smith & Munn 2005). The inclusion of a Chinese person in the jury pool was discussed and debated in the Legislative Council and was supported by a majority vote (Duff et al. 1990). However, Chinese names remained a rarity on the List for the next couple of decades: the 1879 List only had 2 Chinese names out of a total of 476 (Hong Kong Government 1879), and the 1880 List had 6 out of a pool of 480 (Hong Kong Government 1880).

The subsequent popularisation of education resulted in an expansion of the jury pool, as education level has been used as a yardstick for gauging potential Chinese jurors' language ability to understand court proceedings. In the 1987 List, about two thirds of the jurors were Chinese, with the rest being largely European, Australasian and North American expatriates (Duff et al. 1990: 888; 1992: 57). As expatriates then represented only between 2% and 3% of the total population, they were apparently over-represented on the list of eligible jurors (Duff et al. 1990, 1992). It was suggested that those Chinese included in the jury pool were more likely to be well-educated middle-class professionals or business people, rather than typical members of the broader Chinese community (Duff et al. 1990, 1992). This obviously arises from the requirement for jurors to possess a sufficient knowledge of the English language to understand the court proceedings. Indeed, the earlier lists, which included the jurors' occupations and residential addresses, show that the majority of the jurors, both expatriates and locals, had occupations such as 'merchant', 'manager', 'company director', 'banker' and 'accountant'. The Jurors List for 1941 (Hong Kong Government 1941), for example, shows that many jurors lived in the most expensive areas in the territory including 'The Peak', 'Conduit Road', 'Repulse Bay', and some even lived in the Peninsula Hotel, the most luxurious hotel in those days (and even to this day). This gave rise to concerns about the principle of 'trial by peers', as those jurors who satisfied the language requirement could hardly be said to represent the peers of the defendants in criminal trials (Duff et al. 1990, 1992), or to represent a cross-section of the community, for that matter.

The expansion of the jury pool and implications for jury comprehension

The expansion of higher education, which started in the late 1980s, has pushed up overall educational attainment in Hong Kong (Wu & Guo 2022). The 2021 census data (Population Census Office 2021) demonstrate that 34.6% of the population aged 15 or above attained tertiary education. Increased education levels have led to a further expansion of the jury pool, consisting of 795,262 people as per the List of Common

Jurors as of 30 September 2020.[2] This represents slightly over 10% of a population of 7.41 million (Population Census Office 2021), as opposed to 0.2% in 1854.

The expanded list now contains primarily Chinese names, interspersed with some expatriate names.[3] Furthermore, Chinese is now a language option in all the levels of courts in Hong Kong, including the High Court, where jury trials are held. However, as mentioned above, since most criminal trials in the High Court are still routinely conducted in English, a sufficient command of the English language is still an essential requirement for potential jurors.

It is important to note that the majority of the local inhabitants have always been Chinese by ethnicity, speaking Cantonese either as their native language or as a *lingua franca*. The latest census shows that 91.6% of the local population is ethnic Chinese, and that 88.2% of the local population is Cantonese speaking, while native English speakers account for only 4.6% (Population Census Office 2021). To qualify as jurors, one must, among other attributes, have 'a sufficient knowledge of the language in which the proceedings are to be conducted to be able to understand the proceedings' (Jury Ordinance, § 4[1c] 1999). To ensure that the Chinese citizens selected for jury service possess sufficient command of English to understand the court proceedings, a high education level is used as a benchmark, specifically matriculation from high school (*HKSAR* v. *Chan Hon Wing* 2021; Law Reform Commission of Hong Kong 2010). The question is: Does this necessarily guarantee Hong Kong jurors' comprehension of courtroom discourse which could be impenetrable to laypersons even with a native command of the English language, as demonstrated in the literature? Will Chinese jurors with insufficient English proficiency be able to benefit from the day-to-day interpretation service provided in English-medium trials in Hong Kong? The rest of this chapter explores these issues.

Court interpreting in Hong Kong and jurors' access to interpretation

Interestingly, while the selection of jurors, particularly in the past, aimed to ensure that they had the ability to understand the court proceedings conducted in English, the vernacular spoken by local litigants appearing in court as defendants and witnesses has always been a language other than English (LOTE), that is, Cantonese or other Chinese dialects. As mentioned above, the local population is predominantly Cantonese speaking, and thus court interpreting has long been an indispensable service in the Hong Kong courts. In the early colonial days, those English-speaking jurors as fact-finders, like the expatriate judges, had to rely on the English rendition in order to understand the witnesses' testimony to ascertain the said facts.

As a result of this, the mode of interpreting used for witness examination is usually consecutive, whereby counsel's questions in English are rendered into Cantonese for the comprehension of the witness, as well as the defendant in the dock. Likewise, the witness's answer in Cantonese is interpreted into English for the English-speaking counsel and judge (as well as English-speaking jurors). The consecutive mode used in court involves the speaker pausing frequently to allow the interpreter to interpret consecutively. This mode is more transparent, as it is conducted in open court and audible to all those present in court and to the recording system if there is one in place.[4] This consecutive mode of interpreting is supplemented by *chuchotage*, which is used exclusively for the defendant in the dock when counsel is addressing the court or the jury, or when the judge is giving instructions to the jury. In cases where a witness elects to give evidence in English, *chuchotage* is also used to keep a Cantonese-speaking defendant informed of the testimony given by the witness. In the consecutive mode, jurors who have a problem understanding counsel's questions in English or the witness's testimony in Cantonese can benefit from the interpretation provided in open court. *Chuchotage*, however, is provided in the simultaneous mode in a whisper, conventionally known as dockside interpreting as it usually conducted with the interpreter standing close to the defendant and without the use of standard electronic simultaneous interpreting (SI) equipment. In the United States, however, many interpreters use portable wireless equipment to enable them to stand at a distance from the defendant and to whisper into a microphone instead of into the ear of the defendant, who receives the interpretation via earphones (Mikkelson 2017). As noted above, in the Hong Kong courts, the consecutive mode is invariably used for witness examination, rendering the entire process audible to jurors and to the recording system in place. In the United States, interpreters sometimes combine both *chuchotage* and CI in witness testimony, whereby questions asked in English are interpreted into the LOTE in *chuchotage* for the NES witness alone and answers given by the witness are interpreted consecutively into English in a voice loud enough for people in the entire courtroom to hear (Mikkelson 2017). This is consistent with my ethnographic observations in the Boston Immigration Court and in the Superior Court of San Francisco County in 2023.[5]

In Hong Kong, according to a serving full-time court interpreter who wishes to remain anonymous, in recent years, a similar wireless device has been utilised by full-time court interpreters for *chuchotage* interpreting. This device enables the interpreter to provide interpretation for the defendant without having to stand or sit by the dock as the defendant can receive the interpretation via a pair of headphones. However, freelance interpreters have the flexibility to choose between using this device and adhering to dockside interpreting. This may be due to the fact that full-time interpreters in Hong Kong have a designated seat in the centre of the courtroom next the court clerk and close to the witness stand, while freelance interpreters do not have such a designated position. As a result, freelance interpreters may feel more comfortable sitting by the dockside whispering the interpretation into the ear of the defendant.[6] In Hong Kong, freelance interpreters work between English (or Cantonese) and other foreign languages or Chinese dialects, while full-time interpreters must have English and Cantonese as their working languages, in addition to any other language they may speak. In other words, full-time and freelance interpreters in Hong Kong differ not only in their employment status but also in their language combinations. A freelance interpreter in an English-medium trial in Hong Kong courts is usually a second interpreter in addition to the regular full-time interpreter in court. This way, the full-time interpreter's rendition between English and Cantonese will be further interpreted by the freelance interpreter into the foreign language or Chinese dialect involved, which is professionally known as relay interpreting.

It must be noted that *chuchotage*, with or without the use of wireless equipment, is opaque and audible only to the defendant for whom the interpretation is provided. Therefore, jurors have no access to the interpretation, even if they have a comprehension problem and are in need of the interpreting service (see Ng 2023 for a detailed discussion of the limitations of *chuchotage* used in the courtroom). In the case of an English-speaking defendant who elects to give evidence, no interpretation will be provided, either in the consecutive or in the *chuchotage* mode. Therefore, jurors will not be able to benefit from the Cantonese interpretation, as there is none. Similarly, in an English-medium trial, when a defendant who speaks neither English nor Cantonese elects to give evidence, the examination of the defendant will be interpreted consecutively between English and the other language directly by the freelance interpreter without Cantonese mediation from the regular full-time interpreter. This is yet another scenario where jurors are not able to benefit from any Cantonese interpretation but have to rely entirely on the questions asked in English and the English interpretation of the defendant's answers given in a foreign language.

The ubiquitous and obligatory presence of a court interpreter in an English-medium trial creates an illusion of a bilingual courtroom, suggesting that participants in the court proceedings in need of interpreting services are able to benefit from all the interpretation provided in court. This, as explained above, is true only in a restricted sense, depending on the mode of interpreting being used. This misconception was unfortunately held even by the presiding judge in the rape case of which some speech segments were used in the study outlined in this book. Extract 4.1 is taken from the transcript of this case, where a juror selected to serve on this trial was asking via the interpreter to be exempted from the service because she was worried about her English ability.

Extract 4.1 Prospective juror addressing judge via interpreter, rape case

Speaker	**SL speech/Interpretation**
JUROR:	法官大人，因為呢我係一個中文老師，我長期都係使用中文，我少用英文。咁我擔心我喺啫整個過程裏頭呢，我係聽唔明囉。<Request made in Cantonese>
INTERPRETER:	Your Lordship, because I am a Chinese eh language teacher. All along I have been eh using eh Chinese as a teaching medium, and very seldom using eh English. Now I'm worried that during the whole process, eh I will not understand some of the questions.
JUDGE:	Well, you will hear them in both languages, Madam.
INTERPRETER:	咁但係呢，係會用雙語呢，你係會聽倒㗎嚅 <Interpretation in Cantonese>
JUROR:	我聽倒？我樂意接受 <Reply in Cantonese>

INTERPRETER: In that case, I am willing to accept that.

JUDGE: And er, I will be summing up at the end of it. But er, that summing up will also be interpreted. So, you have a chance to hear it in both languages again.

In Extract 4.1, the judge's response to the prospective juror's request to be exempted is obviously misleading. He reassures the potential juror that she will hear the evidence as well as the judge's summing-up in both Chinese and English with the assistance of the court interpreter. The judge is right in so far as interpreting of testimony provided in the consecutive mode is concerned. As the judge's summing-up is interpreted in *chuchotage* for the defendant, inaccessible to the jury, jurors will not be able to hear it in both languages as alleged by the judge. Unwittingly the judge is telling only part of the truth, certainly not the whole truth.

Since the Hong Kong courts are not fully bilingual from jurors' perspective, comprehension issues for jurors as both L2 speakers of the English language and laypersons in the judicial process remain real and substantive, as will be demonstrated in the following sections.

Research on jury comprehension in pre-handover Hong Kong

The first study to shed light on the issue of jury comprehension in Hong Kong was conducted by Duff et al. (1990, 1992). This self-report survey study interviewed 58 individuals who had served as jurors within three years prior to their participation in the survey. The respondents consisted of both expatriates and locals, with 80% indicating that they preferred to speak Cantonese at home. Some respondents admitted that their English was not good enough to understand the proceedings; one English-speaking respondent said that he could not hold even a simple conversation with two of his fellow jurors and wondered how much they had understood of the proceedings. Another respondent expressed surprise over the Cantonese-speaking jurors' limited understanding of English and had to explain to them the meaning of words not limited to legal terms (Duff et al. 1992: 84). One may ask how the deliberations were carried out among the jurors when some of them were not able to communicate with their English-speaking fellow members in English. Would it make those with insufficient English proficiency more suggestible or susceptible to pressure from the English-speaking members if their votes differed? The results of the study indicated that a third of the respondents admitted to experiencing varying degrees of difficulty in comprehending the evidence, the legal terminology and the language of the court. The written responses by some of the jurors, in particular, demonstrated serious problems in their ability to express themselves in English. This led the researchers to conclude that a significant proportion of jurors have some difficulty in understanding the English language (Duff et al. 1992: 84). They suggested that the jurors might not have a sufficient knowledge of English to understand the court proceedings (Duff et al. 1992). It is interesting, if not disturbing, to note that among the respondents who admitted difficulty in following the evidence, close to 80% were members of juries which convicted the defendants. About 75% of the respondents who admitted varying degrees of difficulty in understanding the evidence and/or the legal language found the defendant guilty (Duff et al. 1992). The researchers thus concluded that many defendants were convicted by juries containing members who did not fully understand the court proceedings (ibid.).

This survey study conducted more than three decades ago pointed to an acute jury comprehension problem in Hong Kong. It can be argued that the use of Chinese in the High Court as an option since the changeover of Hong Kong's sovereignty in 1997 has partly resolved the communication problem arising from jurors' insufficient command of English. However, to this day, jury trials conducted in Chinese in the High Court have accounted for only a small percentage, as noted above. English in lieu of Chinese is chosen for a trial either because it is before an expatriate English-speaking judge or because the prosecution and/or the defence counsel do not speak Chinese.

A local television programme which explored the issue of jury comprehension in Hong Kong in 1996 (Lee 1996),[7] one year before the end of the British colonial rule, revealed a serious comprehension problem of serving jurors and people eligible for jury service. The programme interviewed individuals with actual jury experience as well as those eligible for jury service. One interviewee, having served as a juror in the Coroner's Court, admitted that she had a problem understanding the medical term 'stillbirth' in a medical doctor's testimony given in English, and she had to look it up in a dictionary as soon as she got home after the first day of the trial. Three jurors outside the High Court building and a few more eligible for jury service were subsequently approached and asked if they understood this medical term and none of them did. It was also revealed that some other medical terms, including 'cardiac attack', 'cardiac arrest' and 'renal failure' were known to very few of them. To test some of the serving jurors' ability to understand legal instructions, an extract of a judge's jury instructions from a past case was read by a native English-speaking news presenter, recorded and played to the jurors outside the High Court building. None of the four jurors understood the meaning of the recording, even after they had listened to the recording for a second time and were shown the script, which read:

> I have given you already what is called the standard direction that it is unsafe to convict on the **uncorroborated evidence** of an **accomplice**. But in this case, I consider it my duty to tell you that if you consider that there in fact is no **corroboration**, then you should **acquit**.

All four were asked to paraphrase the meaning of the audio recording, but none of them were able to make sense of it. Specifically, the interviewees were asked about the meanings of individual legal terms including 'accomplice', 'corroboration/corroborated evidence' and 'acquit', and all of them admitted that they did not understand the meaning. The programme also revealed two other trials that involved jurors asking for interpreting services or for the judge to explain some legal terms in Chinese, resulting in the dismissal of the juries (Lee 1996).

Due to the continued use of English as a dominant language in jury trials, jury comprehension remains a real issue in the post-colonial Hong Kong society, which is corroborated by anecdotal evidence as illustrated in the following section.

Jury comprehension in post-colonial Hong Kong: Cases in point

This section reviews some court cases involving potential jury comprehension problems. These include jurors asking to be excused on the grounds of 'poor English' or being excused during the process of oath/affirmation making as they demonstrated problems pronouncing some of the words on the standard oath/affirmation. Since the inclusion of potential jurors in the List of Common Jurors is based solely on education level and no tests have been administered to determine their level of proficiency in English, the jury oath or affirmation is often used as a yardstick to test selected jurors' English proficiency (Cheung 2012: 87). However, some argue that problematic pronunciation or self-proclaimed inadequacy in English proficiency might be convenient excuses for potential jurors to avoid this civic duty (Cheung 2012). On the other hand, those who do not ask to be exempted cannot be presumed to have no problems with their English proficiency. They might consider it a loss of face to admit any inadequacy in their English proficiency, or otherwise might overestimate their English proficiency or underestimate the complexities of courtroom discourse. There are cases where jurors' comprehension problems, real or perceived, are advanced as a ground of appeal.

Jurors being excused or asking to be excused before a trial

With the exception of the courts in the United States, where jurors are made to answer questions from parties during the *voir dire* process as discussed in Chapter 2, jurors in other common law courts are silent participants and rarely have to speak out in court, thus rendering it difficult to assess their English proficiency from their spoken English. In the case of Hong Kong, the jury foreperson elected by their fellow members as the spokesperson is presumably the most competent English speaker of the jury. The only occasion on which all the jurors are heard speaking in English is when they take their jury oath or affirmation in English. The following oath and affirmation are used when empanelling jurors in Hong Kong. Jurors may choose whichever version as appropriate.

> Jury oath:
>
> I (name) swear by **Almighty** God that I will give a true **verdict** in this case **according** to the **evidence**.
>
> Jury affirmation:
>
> I (name) **solemnly, sincerely** and truly **affirm** that I will give a true **verdict** in this case **according** to the **evidence**.

The moment jurors take their oath/affirmation is usually a moment of revelation about their English proficiency, assuming that there is no pretence on the part of the jurors concerned. In the two jury trials where I was allowed access to the recordings, most of the jurors were found to struggle with their pronunciation of the boldfaced words in the jury oath/affirmation cited above (see also Ng 2016, 2018.).

This observation is corroborated by a high-profile bribery trial in which a former Chief Executive of the Hong Kong Special Administrative Region (equivalent to the Governor in the colonial era), Mr Donald Tsang, stood as the defendant (*HKSAR* v. *Tsang Yam Kuen Donald* 2015). In this case, a juror had to be replaced after she had mispronounced 'verdict' as 'v dict', 'solemnly' as 'solely' and 'affirm' as 'afim' when taking her affirmation. The judge had to demonstrate to her the correct pronunciation of those words and to ask her to repeat after him. Seeing that the juror was nonetheless not able to pronounce those words correctly, the judge decided to excuse her, stressing the importance for jurors to possess a sufficient knowledge of the English language in order to understand the proceedings (Lau 2017; see also Ng 2016, 2018).

Moreover, there have been jurors who, having been selected for jury service, asked to be excused in court, claiming not to possess the required proficiency in English, as demonstrated in the case cited in Extract 4.1 above. While some requests were accepted, others were rejected. For example, in a murder case in which a university professor was charged with murdering his wife (*HKSAR* v. *Khaw Kim Sun* 2017), the empanelling of a jury of nine members was a real challenge for the court, as many of the jurors selected asked to be exempted for various reasons including inadequate English proficiency. Those who were able to communicate with the judge in English, including one holding a Master's degree, were not excused from service, even though the juror in question told the court that his Master's degree was in Chinese literature ('*Shuoshi ye cheng yingwen cha*' 2018).

The jury who failed to understand 'acquit'

The court might be sceptical about jurors' claim of inadequate English proficiency, suspecting this to be a convenient excuse, but other cases have demonstrated very real comprehension problems. This is particularly worrying when the problem is not made known to the court until after the trial has reached the final stage, rather than during the jury empanelling process or at an early stage of the trial. For example, in a rape trial (*HKSAR* v. *Henry Tse* 2016), the jury returned to court during deliberations to ask the judge for a Chinese translation of 'acquit' ('*Chushi she jian an*' 2017), one of the fundamental legal concepts in jury deliberations. Since the presiding judge did not speak Chinese, he was not able to provide a Chinese translation. Instead, he explained to the jury that 'acquit' means to find the defendant 'not guilty', while 'convict' is the same as finding the defendant 'guilty'. One may wonder if the judge had sufficiently explained the terms in his earlier instructions to the jury, be it at the beginning of the trial or during the summing-up stage at the end of the trial. It might well be the case that the judge did explain such terms, but his message did not reach the jury, possibly arising from voice projection problems (physically and/or discursively) as suggested by Heffer (2018), which will be further discussed in Chapter 6.

Convictions overturned based on concerns about jury comprehension

In other cases, no issues surrounding jury comprehension were raised at any stage of the trial, yet jurors' comprehension was subsequently cited as a basis for appeal. For instance, in *HKSAR* v. *Lai She Hung* (2004), the inconsistency in the verdicts returned by the jury fuelled speculation that the jury had failed to comprehend the judge's instructions regarding the verdicts to be returned. Moreover, a review of the transcript of the court proceedings indicated an apparent difficulty that the jury foreman experienced in communicating with the court and in understanding the meaning of a 'majority verdict'. In this case, the defendant was charged with one count of false imprisonment (Count 1) and two counts of rape (Counts 2 and 3). It was alleged that the defendant forced the complainant to stay in his flat (subject matter of Count 1), where he had sexual intercourse with her twice on the same day without her consent (subject matter of Counts 2 and 3). Following a trial in the High Court before a judge and a jury of seven members, the defendant was acquitted of Counts 1 and 2 but was convicted of Count 3. The defendant appealed against the conviction based on the grounds of inconsistency in the verdicts and the jury's confusion over the verdicts, specifically the jury foreman's problem with his understanding of the meaning of a majority verdict (*HKSAR* v. *Lai She Hung* 2005).

With regard to the first ground of appeal, the counsel for the applicant argued in the Court of Appeal (CA) in this way:

> It is difficult, if not impossible, in the circumstances, to follow the jury's reasoning when they disbelieved the complainant in relation to counts 1 and 2, which formed the gravamen of her complaint, but yet relied on the same witness in relation to count 3.
>
> (*HKSAR* v. *Lai She Hung* 2005)

The CA reviewed the trial judge's instructions to the jury to see if the jury had been properly and adequately instructed as regards the verdicts to be returned, and concluded that the trial judge had given fair and clear directions to the jury in his summing-up. Specifically, the CA noted that 'the apparent inconsistency in the verdicts' was something the trial judge had anticipated and sought to avoid in his summing up 'of paramount fairness and clarity' (*HKSAR* v. *Lai She Hung 2005*). Below is an extract (Extract 4.2) of the relevant directions as cited in the CA's judgment:

> **Extract 4.2**
>
> All **permutations** are, as a matter of law, available to you. You decide in giving these three counts your separate consideration. **But you may think – and again this is entirely a matter for you – that as the case has been presented to you on the issues that are laid before**

> **you, and where the central issue in the case is one of consent – 'Did this lady consent to what happened or did she not?** Did she consent to remain in the flat? Did she or did she not consent to have sex with the defendant?' – then, in practice, you may think – and it is entirely a matter for you – that these three counts stand or fall together; guilty to all or not guilty to all.
>
> (emphasis added)

The essence of the trial judge's instructions regarding the verdicts on the three counts is that, theoretically, the jury could return a different verdict for each count. However, in practice, it might appear to be more reasonable for the jury to find the defendant guilty to all or to none of the charges. There is no knowing, however, whether the judge's message was effectively communicated to the jury, even though the judge used questions to guide their deliberations. The message, laden with legalistic language manifested in the use of formal terminology (for example, 'permutations') and complex syntactic structure, specifically the boldfaced sentence, might not have projected well to a jury unfamiliar with the legal register and discourse.

While one can only speculate on the jury's comprehension of these directions, the jury's confusion over the meaning of 'a verdict upon which at least five of you have agreed' might be more telling about the jury foreman's English proficiency. This aggravated the CA's concern about the jury's understanding of the directions, as the court observed in *HKSAR* v. *Lai She Hung* (2005):

> **Extract 4.3**
>
> Whether or not the obvious wisdom of these directions fell on deaf ears because they were not fully comprehended by the jury is difficult to say.... What seems plain, whatever may have been the reason for it, is that **this particular jury had the greatest difficulty in following explicit directions** which had been given to them about the nature of majority verdicts, supplemented, as these directions were, by a written form setting out the questions they would be asked at the time they returned their verdicts.
>
> (emphasis added)

Indeed, the jury foreman did demonstrate an immense difficulty in his understanding of the meaning of 'a verdict upon which at least five of you have agreed'. As a result, what was expected to be a brief exchange of a few lines between the court clerk and the jury foreman expanded into a lengthy interaction of 139 turns. During this time, both the judge and the defence counsel intervened to help rephrase the court's questions and clarify the jury foreman's answers, but their efforts were in vain. The following is an extract of the transcript as cited in the CA's judgment (Extract 4.4):

Extract 4.4

CLERK: May the foreman please stand. On the 1st count of false imprisonment against the accused, Lai She-hung, have you reached your verdict upon which at least five of you have agreed?

FOREMAN: No.

COURT: Very well, let's go to the next count. Members of the jury, have you reached a verdict on any count upon which at least …

FOREMAN: I'm sorry, maybe I misunderstand …

COURT: Yes.

FOREMAN: … the question, so …

COURT: Have you reached a verdict on the 1st count of false imprisonment upon which at least five of you are agreed?

FOREMAN: No.

COURT: Very well. Have you reached a verdict …

DEFENCE COUNSEL: Well, I'm sorry, my Lord.

COURT: Yes.

DEFENCE COUNSEL: I heard some of the jurors saying 'Yes'.

COURT: Ah. Well …

Thinking that the foreman might have a problem with his understanding of the phrase 'at least five', the court, at the suggestion of the defence counsel, rephrased it to 'five or more', which, however, did not seem to help. As it turned out, the jury had already reached a not-guilty verdict of 6 to 1 in respect of Count 1, yet the foreman repeatedly told the court that the jury had not reached a verdict upon which at least five of the jurors agreed. The later part of the transcript shows that the foreman might have misunderstood 'a verdict upon which at least five of you have agreed' to mean a verdict whereby at least five of them 'agreed to convict'. This is because in respect of Count 1, only one juror agreed that the defendant was guilty. This observation was supported by the jury foreman's answer to the court's question about Count 3, for which the jury had reached a verdict upon which 6 of the jurors agreed that the defendant was guilty. (See Extract 4.5 below.)

Extract 4.5

FOREMAN: For the 3rd count, our answer is five or more of us have agreed.

COURT: I see. Very well. On the 3rd count then.

CLERK:	Okay. On the 3rd count of rape against the accused, Lai She-hung, have you reached your verdict upon which at least or more of five of you have agreed to?
FOREMAN:	Yes.
CLERK:	Is the verdict unanimous?
FOREMAN:	No.
CLERK:	By what majority have you arrived at the verdict?
FOREMAN:	Six to one.
CLERK:	What's the verdict?
FOREMAN:	Guilty.

Apparently, the jury foreman had wrongly taken 'agreed' to mean 'agreed that the defendant was guilty'. That is why the answer this time was 'Yes'. In other words, 'agreed' meant 'agreed to convict' for the jury foreman. Since the jury foreman's answer to the other two counts were negative, the court asked the jury to continue their deliberations in respect of these two offences. At this point the jury foreman asked for the court's permission to present the jury's verdict in a different way. (See Extract 4.6 below.)

Extract 4.6

FOREMAN:	If they - - in order to eliminate any ambiguity, if, my Lord, you may allow us to let you know about how many number of 'yes' and how many number of 'no' …
COURT:	Yes.
FOREMAN:	… then definitely it will be …
COURT:	All right. …
FOREMAN:	… the answer.
COURT:	Don't tell me what your verdict is but are you unanimous on the 1st count?
FOREMAN:	No.
COURT:	All right. Well, in what way …
FOREMAN:	Proportional.
COURT:	… are you split on the 1st count?
FOREMAN:	One to six.
COURT:	One to six.
FOREMAN:	One 'yes' and six 'no'.
COURT:	All right, well, I can accept a verdict of six to one. Can you tell me your verdict? Is it guilty or not guilty on the 1st count?

FOREMAN: Not guilty.

COURT: Not guilty. By a majority of six to one? Very well. Now, in respect of the 2nd count, to continue doing it in your way, are you unanimous?

FOREMAN: No.

COURT: And in what way are you split?

FOREMAN: Three 'yes' and four 'no'.

COURT: Well, no …

DEFENCE COUNSEL: No, no, no

COURT: … that is not a verdict that I can accept, and so what I'm going to do, in those circumstances, is to invite you to continue your deliberations to see if you can reach a verdict in respect of that.

Now, is there any assistance that I can give you in respect of that 2nd count?

FOREMAN: I think for the members of jury we are quite - - we have decided the verdict. If you may ask me 'guilty' or 'not guilty' then I give you the answer.

DEFENCE COUNSEL: No.

COURT: Well, you see, I can't, because you've told me that you're split 3:4 so that is not a verdict that I can accept either way.

For the court, a verdict of 1 to 6 is no different from one of 6 to 1. They are both valid verdicts that can be accepted by the court, be it a verdict of guilty or not guilty, which apparently the jury foreman failed to appreciate. Extract 4.6 above also demonstrates that the jury did not know a verdict of 3 to 4 in whatever direction could not be accepted by the court, as the foreman told the court that the jury had decided on the verdict. Presumably, in this case, the judge would have instructed the jury about the acceptable verdicts before they retired for deliberations. The appeal advanced on the inconsistency in the verdicts and the jury foreman's confusion about the verdicts was subsequently allowed, and the conviction in respect of Count 3 was quashed. No retrial was ordered.

Jurors' request to access *chuchotage* interpretation

As noted above, despite interpreting between Chinese and English being a routine service in trials conducted in English, jurors do not have access to the *chuchotage* interpretation of monologues or of testimony given in English. In the trial of *HKSAR* v. *Chan Hon Wing* (2015), the jury's need to access the *chuchotage* interpretation provided for the defendant was first vocalised.

In this trial, the defendant faced three counts of drug-related offences. The trial was conducted in English but all the evidence was given in Cantonese, as in any typical trial conducted in English in Hong Kong. CI and *chuchotage* were used at different phases of the trial. At a later stage of the trial, the jury requested access to the Cantonese *chuchotage* of counsel's closing addresses and the judge's summing-up. Headphones were subsequently provided for some jurors in need of the service to listen to the Cantonese interpretation provided in *chuchotage*, while others listened to the original speech in English. The defendant was ultimately found guilty and sentenced to 26 years in prison.

This case provides further evidence of jurors' comprehension issues and highlights the need for Chinese jurors to access language assistance in court proceedings conducted in English. Unfortunately, the unprecedented arrangement for jurors to access the *chuchotage* interpretation ended in an appeal at the Court of Appeal (CA) and the Court of Final Appeal (CFA). The rulings and conflicting arguments of the two appellate courts and their implications for court interpreting will be examined and discussed in Chapter 7.

Summary

This chapter has reviewed the operation of the jury system in Hong Kong from its early colonial days to the present post-colonial times. It has explored the issue of jury comprehension in this linguistic landscape that is fundamentally different from most other common law jurisdictions. Juries in the early colonial days were composed of only expatriate English-speaking residents and a small number of Chinese elites, making them the least representative of a cross-section of the community. The expansion of the jury *venire* has, on the one hand, improved the representativeness of the jury institution in Hong Kong. On the other hand, this gives rise to a cause for concern as to whether Chinese jurors with English as their L2 have a sufficient command of the language to comprehend courtroom discourse which even L1 speakers find difficult to understand. Findings of an earlier study (Duff et al. 1990, 1992) have highlighted this as a worrying problem, corroborated by anecdotal evidence including appeals advanced on grounds related to jury comprehension problems. Besides, despite court interpreting being a *sine qua non* in English-medium trials even to this day, jurors with inadequate English proficiency do not have full access to the interpreting service, due to the use of *chuchotage* as one of the common modes of interpreting in court. The *HKSAR* v. *Chan Hon Wing* (2015) case further highlights the jury comprehension problem in the Hong Kong courtroom and underscores the need for full language assistance for jurors. To further explore jury comprehension issues in the special context of Hong Kong, an empirical study was conducted. The next chapter describes the conduct of this study and presents its quantitative results.

Notes

1. The *Carrian* fraud case, which lasted a total of 180 trial days.
2. The List of Common Jurors is compiled every two years. The List is not available online or published in the *Government Gazette* as in the old days, but is available for public inspection in the Jury Clerk's Office in the High Court Building. I made a visit to the Jury Clerk's Office on 26 May 2022 to obtain the latest information, including the total number of jurors on the List.
3. See note 2 above.
4. Following the installation of the Digital Audio Recording and Transcription System (DARTS) in Hong Kong courts in 1995, both the original and the interpreted versions of the courtroom discourse are recorded save interpretation provided in *chuchotage*, which cannot be picked up by the system.
5. These field trips were supported by the Harvard-Yenching Visiting Scholars Program 2022–2023, which funded my 10-month visit at Harvard University to work on this book project.
6. My two visits to the High Court of Hong Kong in March and in early August 2024 confirmed this observation. The defendants in both trials were non-locals speaking Bangladesh and Zulu, respectively, and therefore both trials involved freelance interpreters at work as second interpreters. The freelance interpreters in both cases were providing dockside interpreting without using any wireless device.
7. This TV programme was re-aired by Television Broadcasts Limited in Hong Kong in February 2022 as an episode of the *News Treasury*.

5

The Study: Data, Methodology and Results

The previous chapter examined the operation of the jury system in Hong Kong, focusing on the challenges of assembling jurors for English-medium trials in a predominantly Chinese society and the importance of ensuring that selected jurors possess the necessary English proficiency to understand court proceedings. The chapter shed light on a concerning issue of comprehension in Hong Kong, which has received limited scholarly attention and warrants further investigation. Against this backdrop, an empirical study was conducted, with an aim to explore the issue of jury comprehension in the unique linguistic landscape of Hong Kong, where jurors often have to listen to trials conducted in a foreign language. Participants in the study were Hong Kong residents eligible for jury service, with or without actual jury experience. Authentic audio recordings of two jury trials were used; participants were asked to listen to recordings extracted from various stages of the two jury trials and to read a written excerpt from a trial transcript before they answered a series of questions designed to assess their comprehension levels (see also Ng 2022). This chapter outlines the methodology and presents the quantitative results obtained from the study. The results of the study are analysed in relation to participants' demographics to identify any correlations between their comprehension levels and backgrounds, including their age, gender, occupation, education level, experience with jury experience, frequency of English use, and so on.

Data and methodology

As outlined in Chapter 3, previous research into jury comprehension has primarily centred on assessing jurors' understanding of jury instructions, with a focus on the legal nature of the language used in those instructions. These studies have typically employed self-report measures, paraphrase tests or mock trials. None of these studies, however, have used authentic audio recordings to evaluate participants' comprehension of actual court proceedings. In contrast, the present study employed a combination of self-rating measures and objective tests to assess prospective jurors' comprehension of selected courtroom discourse. More importantly, the audio recordings used in the study featured court participants speaking in their own voices, providing an authentic representation of the language used in court proceedings.

Access to data and ethical approval

The data utilised in this study were derived from two English-language jury trials, one involving a murder case and the other a rape case. These trials were part of a collection of nine trials that I had the privilege of accessing. In 2009, as a researcher and former court interpreter, I obtained special permission from the then High Court Registrar of the Hong Kong Judiciary to access the audio recordings of these nine trials. This permission was granted for the purpose of my earlier research projects on court interpreting and for training purposes.

In 2017, a grant application was submitted to the Research Grants Council (RGC) of Hong Kong for a project aimed at examining the issue of jury comprehension in Hong Kong. The project proposed utilising data from the two jury trials. In compliance with the research ethics committee of my home university, a request was made for permission to use the data for the project, and approval was subsequently granted by the court.[1] In the same year, the project proposal received a significant research grant from the RGC of Hong Kong.

Selection of data for the study

The data extracted from both trials include speech segments of the judge's instructions to the jury, the prosecution counsel's opening address, and the judge's summing-up. The murder case also includes the examination-in-chief and cross-examination of a local expert witness testifying in English. As explained in Chapter 4, jurors in court have no access to the *chuchotage* of legal monologues and testimony given in English, as interpretation provided in this mode is audible only to the defendant in the dock. Without being able to benefit from the interpretation provided in the *chuchotage* mode, jurors' comprehension of the English speech is therefore important and hence its inclusion in the data. No witness examination was extracted from the rape case as it did not involve any witness testimony in English. All the witnesses testified in Cantonese in this case, mediated by a court interpreter in the consecutive mode. The variety of speech acts and delivery styles on the recordings enables comparisons and contrasts to be made in the identification of factors impeding jurors' comprehension. The speech segments range from 1m 12s to 4m 40s in length. For comparative purposes, a written text of 225 words was also extracted from the transcript of the murder trial to compare participants' reading comprehension and listening comprehension levels (see Section C of the study questionnaire in Appendix 1).

The questionnaire

The study questionnaire (Appendix 1) consisted of three sections. Section A was designed to collect participants' demographic information so as to identify any correlations between the independent variables (including participants' age, education, occupation, previous jury experience and so on) and the dependent variable, that is, their comprehension levels of the courtroom discourse. This section also asked participants about their experience of living in an English-speaking country and how often they speak and/or write in English at home, at work and when communicating with friends. Participants were also asked to rate their English proficiency in writing, listening and speaking. This section had 30 questions in total.

Section B measured participants' listening comprehension and consisted of 72 questions, 50 of which related to the murder trial and the remaining 22 to the rape case. Of the 72 questions, 20 asked participants for a self-evaluation of their listening comprehension of the speech segments, as well as the perceived factors behind any comprehension problem. A set of five response options, ranging from 'completely' to 'not at all', were provided for participants to rate their understanding of the speech. Participants were also provided with a list of suggested factors to explain the comprehension problems including 'the speaker's accent' and 'the speaker spoke too fast', or they could give their own answers. Multiple answers were allowed.

The remaining 52 mark-carrying questions consisted of 22 multiple-choice questions and 30 open questions. Each question carried 1 mark and thus the full mark for the listening comprehension section was 52. Contrary to the open questions which required participants to provide their own answers (in either English or Chinese), the multiple-choice questions allowed participants to select from a set of three or four response options. To reduce the chance of pure guessing, an option of 'not sure' was also included, avoiding the forced-choice response format without such an option adopted by the majority of research (Baguley et al. 2020). The use of open questions can provide a more accurate measure of participants' comprehension. In open questions, participants are required to paraphrase or explain their understanding, thus limiting the possibility of guessing or relying on response options, unlike multiple-choice questions that may provide clues. As Charrow and Charrow (1979) point out, participants can only paraphrase or explain what they comprehend. However, the inability to provide a correct answer to an open question does not necessarily indicate a lack of comprehension but rather a failure to remember the information (Ogloff & Rose 2005). To aid participants' memory, pens and paper were provided so that they could take notes, mimicking the practice of jurors during trials. It is believed that incorporating a combination of both open and closed questions helps strike an optimal balance between participants' guessing and genuine understanding while maximising data for analysis.

Section C, designed to compare participants' reading comprehension with their listening comprehension competence, required them to read a text and then answer five questions, including one self-evaluation question and four mark-carrying questions. All four mark-carrying questions in Section C were open questions.

The charges facing the defendants in the two jury trials and the particulars of the offences, as well as the topics of the recordings (e.g. a judge's jury instructions, or counsel's opening address) were provided on the questionnaire in Sections B and C as background information for participants.

Sampling and conduct of the study

Snowball sampling was used for this study, with participants recruited through social network groups and friend referrals. Over 70 people signed up for the study via an online link created for this purpose. A total of 53 people eventually took part in the test.

As part of the standard procedure, an informed consent form for adults was designed, outlining the study's purpose, procedures, remuneration details and confidentiality measures for personal data. Each participant signed this form before beginning the test. Additionally, a declaration form was signed and dated by each participant, confirming their eligibility for jury service and their agreement not to disclose the contents of the study.

The test was conducted within a language laboratory, with six group sessions lasting approximately one and a half hours each. Following the completion of all the sessions, the questionnaires were scanned and saved on a secure server. To streamline the analysis process, the questionnaire was later transferred to a Google form, and the responses were manually entered into it. The data from the 53 completed forms were then exported as Excel spreadsheets for further analysis.

Results of the study

Demographics of participants

Table 5.1 summarises the major demographic information of the participants in this study.

Table 5.1 Major demographics of participants

	Number	Percentage
Age		
21–29	36	67.92%
30–39	4	7.55%
40–49	10	18.87%
50–59	3	5.66%
Gender		
Male	15	28.30%
Female	38	71.70%
Education		
Doctorate	3	5.66%
Master's degree	14	26.41%
Bachelor's degree	35	66.04%
Associate degree	1	1.89%

Table 5.1 (continued)

	Number	Percentage
Place of birth		
Hong Kong	46	86.79%
Mainland China	6	11.32%
Australia	1	1.89%
First language (L1)		
Cantonese	53	100%
Length of stay in English-speaking countries		
0–under 3 months	33	62.26%
3 months–under a year	9	16.98%
1 year or more	11	20.76%
Occupation		
Accounting and consultancy	5	9.43%
Administration and marketing	20	37.74%
Architecture and engineering	3	5.66%
Culture, media and social work	5	9.43%
Education, editing and translation	15	28.31%
Others	5	9.43%
Usage of English	See results in Figures 5.1 and 5.2	

Age, gender, education, dominant language, English exposure and occupation

The 53 participants comprise 15 males and 38 females, aged between 21 and 59, with education levels ranging from associate to doctoral degrees, all therefore meeting the education-level requirement for jury service. All of them reported speaking Cantonese as their first language (L1), although not all of them were born in Hong Kong. The majority (62.26%) had never lived in an English-speaking country for a period of three months or longer, while the remaining 37.74% had done so for varying durations from 4 to 72 months. Most of the participants worked in the field of administration and marketing, followed by education, editing and translation.

English usage

Participants were also asked about their use of English at home, at work and for communicating with their friends. The majority (73.58%) of participants reported 'never' or 'rarely' speaking English at home, and none reported 'always' speaking English at home. On the other hand, participants reported more frequent English usage with friends and at work (see Figure 5.1).

In contrast, participants reported a much higher use of written English at work and for communication with friends (see Figure 5.2). This is understandable because English is used in many workplaces as a primary means of formal written

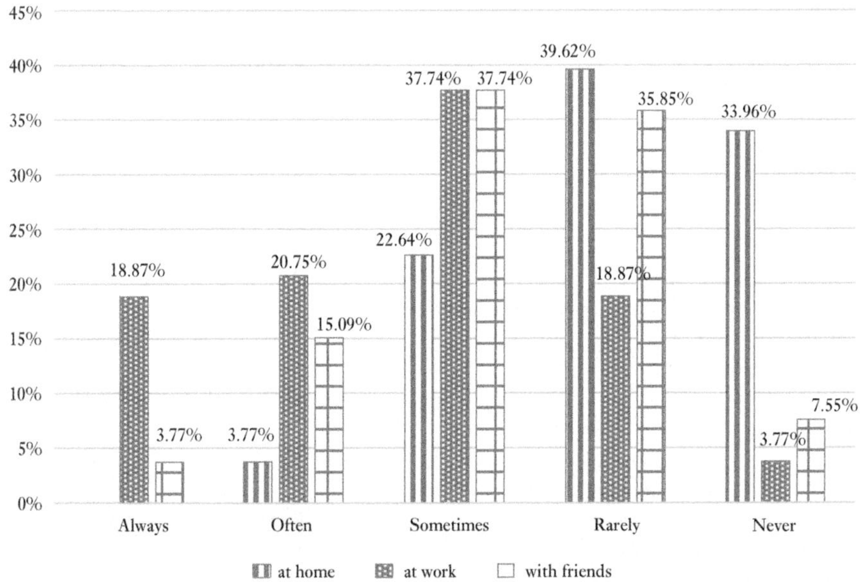

Figure 5.1 Speaking English at home, at work and with friends

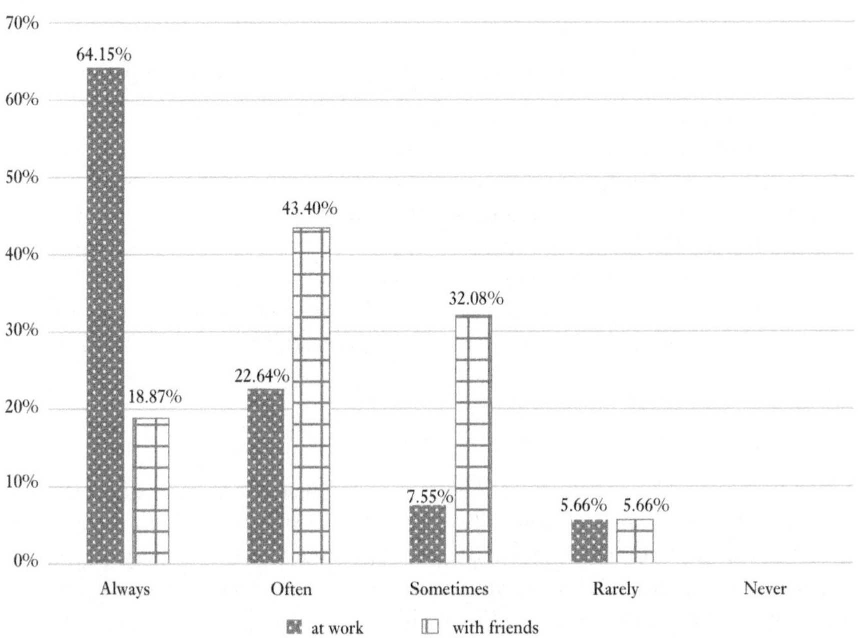

Figure 5.2 Writing in English at work and with friends

communication. None of the participants indicated that they 'never' had to write in English at work.

Jury experience

Of the 53 participants, 18 reported having previously been summoned for jury service, and seven had actual jury experience. Of the seven participants with actual jury experience, five indicated that the trials were conducted in English and the other two in Cantonese. Of the five participants with jury experience in English-medium trials, only one (20%) claimed to have understood all the legal speeches completely. The rest indicated varying degrees of understanding of the different types of legal speeches: three participants reported comprehending the jury instructions 'to a great extent', while one understood them 'somewhat'; two participants reported understanding the counsel speeches 'to a great extent', and two others understood them 'somewhat'; none of these experienced jurors reported understanding the legal speeches 'very little' or 'not at all'.

In the five English trials, four were reported to have involved witnesses testifying in English. When asked how much they had understood the testimony given in English, two reported having understood the testimony 'to a great extent', while the other two indicated their comprehension as 'somewhat'.

As explained in Chapter 4, where witnesses testify in Cantonese via an interpreter, jurors can benefit from the Cantonese interpretation of counsel's questions asked in English. When asked how often they had to rely on the Cantonese interpretation to understand counsel's questions asked in English, one picked 'often' and another 'rare', while the other two reported having to do so 'sometimes'.

Of the five English trials, Cantonese was reported to have been used in four out of the five cases during verdict deliberations. The lone case in which English was used presumably involved one or more English-speaking jurors, and thus the deliberations could not be held in Cantonese.

With regard to the verdict returned by the juries in these five cases, four guilty and one not-guilty verdicts were purportedly returned. It might be argued that in the four guilty cases, the defendants were convicted by some jurors who did not fully understand the legal instructions or testimony given in English. This seems to corroborate with the findings of Duff et al. (1990, 1992). The following section presents the comprehension results of the study.

Listening comprehension

As explained above, Section B had 52 mark-carrying questions (36 questions for the murder trial and 16 for the rape case) and each question carried one mark. The comprehension rates for the murder and the rape trial are 36.48% and 61.32%, respectively – the difference is substantial, and the overall average listening comprehension level for the two cases combined is 41.50%. Figure 5.3 presents the participants' comprehension levels of the eight speech segments from both cases.

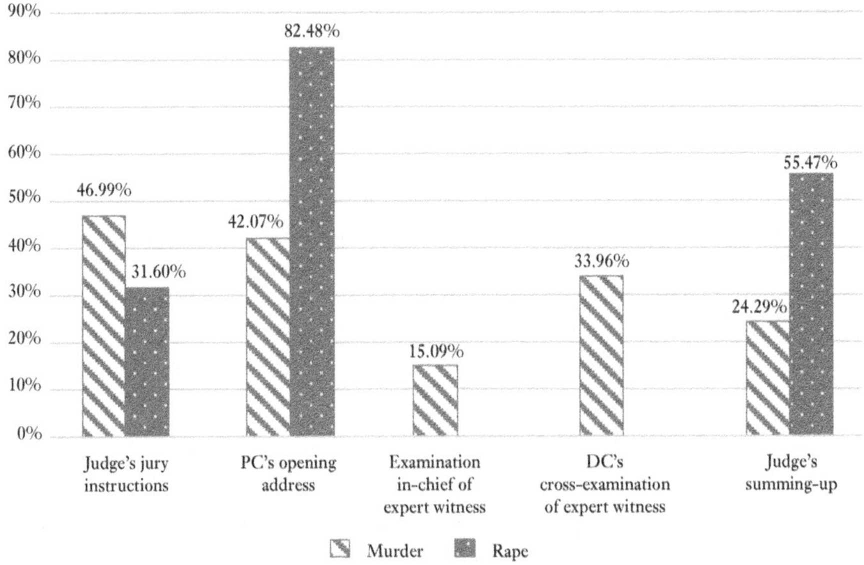

Figure 5.3 Listening comprehension results of the eight speech segments

A qualitative analysis of the features of the speech segments and their potential impact on participants' comprehension will be conducted Chapter 6.

In terms of question type, the participants achieved a significantly higher average accuracy rate of 55.40% for the 22 multiple-choice questions compared with the 30 open questions, which only yielded an average accuracy rate of 35.85%. The higher accuracy rate for multiple-choice questions is not unexpected, though. As mentioned earlier, apart from the possibility of guessing, the provided response options might have facilitated the participants' recollection and comprehension abilities.

Reading comprehension

Section C of the questionnaire included a transcribed text excerpt from the judge's summing-up in the murder case, followed by five questions. The comprehension rate for this written text reached 86.79%, which is strikingly higher than the average listening comprehension rate, although all the questions in this section are open questions. The comprehension of the audio recording segment extracted from an earlier part of the same summing-up in contrast exhibits a significantly lower comprehension rate of 24.29%. This indicates that the participants' reading comprehension ability is much stronger than their listening comprehension skills.

The finding that the participants demonstrated higher reading comprehension rates compared to their listening comprehension rates is largely in line with expectations. This result aligns with Kurita's (2012: 35) suggestion that listening comprehension scores tend to be lower than reading comprehension scores. This could be attributed to the real-time acoustic nature of spoken language. L2 users in particular may recognise a word in its written form but struggle to do so in its spoken form. This is corroborated by Altenberg's (2005) study, which revealed that L2 English learners with Spanish as their first language (L1) had difficulties in segmenting speech in English based on acoustic-phonetic cues and performed significantly worse than native English speakers.

Scores of participants

The listening and reading comprehension questions together generate a total score of 56. Figure 5.4 illustrates the distribution of the scores, with the x-axis showing the scores and the y-axis indicating the number of participants attaining the corresponding scores. For example, two participants scored 12 marks and one obtained the highest score of 39.

Table 5.2 summarises the descriptive statistics generated from the dataset of the 53 participants' individual scores, with the mean and the standard deviation rounded off to two decimal places.

Table 5.2 shows that the mean (average score), the median (the middlemost value of the scores when ordered from smallest to largest) and the mode (the score that occurs most frequently) are fairly close: 25.68, 26 and 23, respectively. This suggests a relatively symmetrical distribution of scores, as demonstrated graphically in the boxplot in Figure 5.5.

The box in Figure 5.5 represents the middle 50% of the dataset. The upper edge of the box (30) corresponds to the upper quartile (Q3), while the lower edge (21) represents the lower quartile (Q1). The interquartile range (IQR) is calculated as the difference between Q3 and Q1, which in this case is nine. This indicates that the

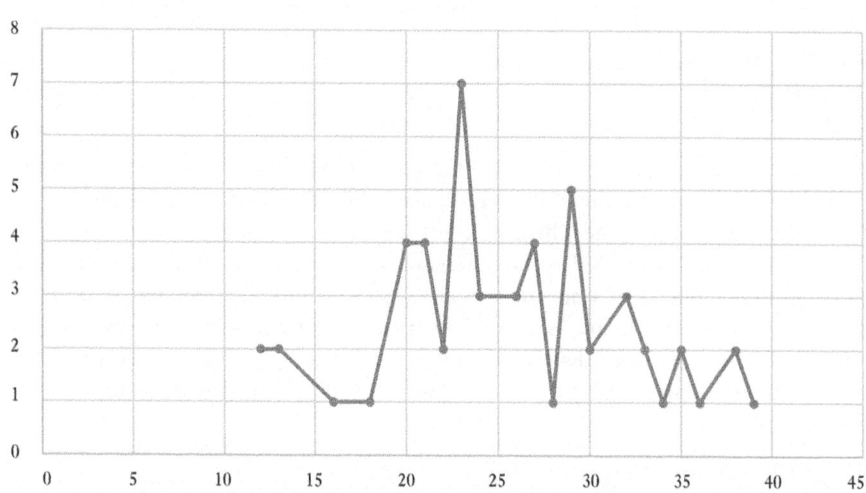

Figure 5.4 Scores of participants

Table 5.2 Descriptive statistics of scores

Count (n)	53
Mean	25.68
Median/Second quartile (Q2)	26
Mode	23
Standard deviation (SD)	6.67
Range	27
Minimum	12
Maximum	39
Lower/First quartile (Q1)	21
Upper/Third quartile (Q3)	30
Interquartile range (IQR)	9

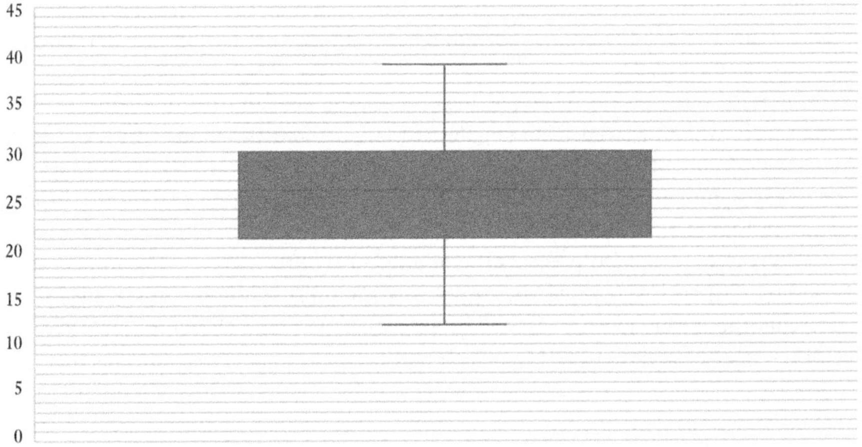

Figure 5.5 Score distribution

middle 50% of the participants scored between 21 and 30, 25% of the participants scored below 21 and another 25% scored above 30. The median (Q2) is located in the middle of the box. The whiskers, represented by T-shapes, indicate the range (27) of the dataset, calculated as the difference between the maximum value (39) and the minimum value (12). The whiskers are approximately the same length on both sides of the box, which suggests a symmetrical or normal bell-shape distribution without outliers. A normal distribution means that that 68% of the scores are within one standard deviation (SD) from the mean (Agresti 2018), that is, 25.68±6.67 in this case.

Comprehension and demographics

This section compares the participants' demographics, including their experience in jury service, with their levels of comprehension.

Comprehension and age group

As shown in Table 5.1, the majority (36) of the participants fall within the age group of 21–29, followed by the 40–49 age group (10). Four are aged between 30 and 39 and three participants belong to the 50–59 age group. The study findings indicate that participants in the 40–49 age group achieved the highest average comprehension rate, scoring 53.13%. The other age groups scored similar rates, ranging narrowly from 43.39% to 45.44% (see Figure 5.6).

Comprehension and gender

In terms of gender, the 15 male participants achieved a slightly higher comprehension level with an average score of 26 out of 56 (46.43%), compared to the comprehension level of 24 out of 56 (42.86%) attained by the 38 female participants. The difference is, however, too small to be of statistical significance, especially given the small sample size.

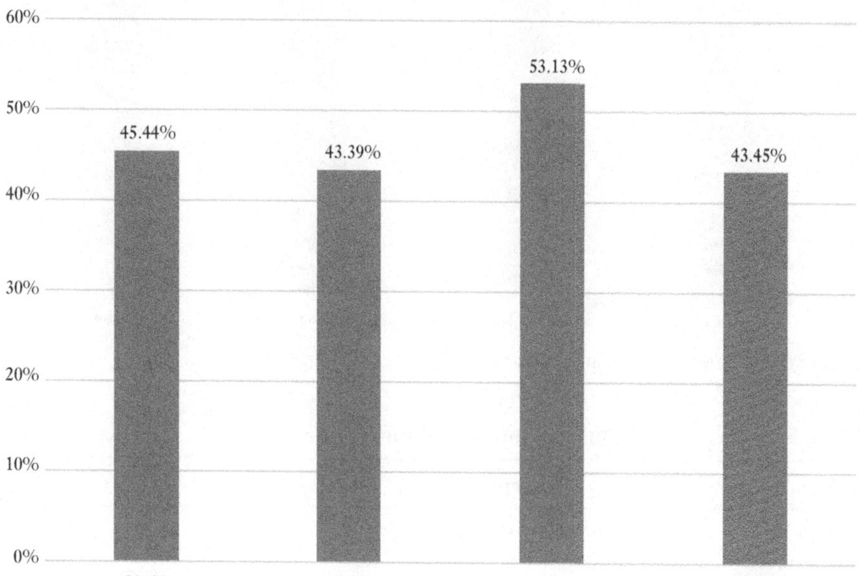

Figure 5.6 Comprehension and age group

Comprehension and education level

With reference to education levels, the findings indicate that participants with a postgraduate degree outperformed those with a Bachelor's degree or lower. However, the average score of the three doctoral degree holders was slightly lower than that of the Master's degree holders (see Figure 5.7).

A Pearson correlation test shows a coefficient of 0.17, which suggests a negligible or very weak correlation between the two variables. This is presumably because individuals eligible for jury service are typically well educated, as noted in Chapter 4. Within a narrow range of education levels, the variation in their comprehension levels is therefore small. As a matter of fact, the participant who scored the highest accuracy rate (69.64%) and the two participants with the lowest score all hold Bachelor's degrees. These results, coupled with the fact that there is only one associate degree holder, renders it difficult to arrive at any conclusion about the correlation between education and comprehension in this study. For the purpose of this analysis, the following magnitude interpretations of correlation coefficients taken from Evans (1996: 146) were adopted (Table 5.3).

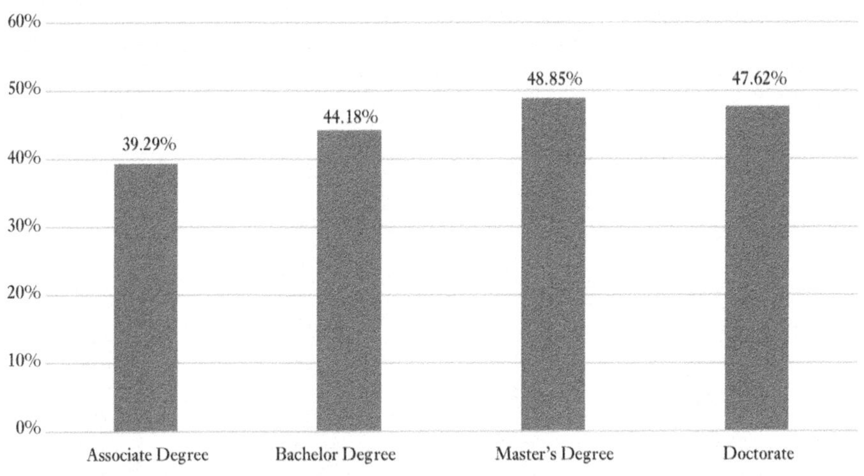

Figure 5.7 Comprehension and education

Table 5.3 Correlation value and interpretation

Value	Interpretation
0.80 to 1.00	Very strong
0.60 to 0.79	Strong
0.40 to 0.59	Moderate
0.20 to 0.39	Weak
0.00 to 0.19	Negligible to very weak

Comprehension and occupation

To facilitate comparison, participants' reported occupations were grouped into six categories: 1) accounting and consultancy, 2) administration and marketing, 3) architecture and engineering, 4) culture, media and social work, 5) education, editing and translation, and 6) others. The 'others' category includes participants indicating their occupations as 'civil servant', 'freelancer' and 'company owner'. Individuals working in the media, culture or social work sectors outperformed those in other categories, achieving an average accuracy rate of 53.93%. Intriguingly, participants in the education, translation and editing category achieved the lowest average comprehension level (40.5%). It might be argued that people working in the media, cultural and social sectors have more exposure to spoken English, whereas those working in the fields of education, editing and translation primarily deal with written English (see Figure 5.8 for a visual representation of these findings). The number of participants in each occupational category is indicated in brackets, with the majority employed in the administration and marketing sector.

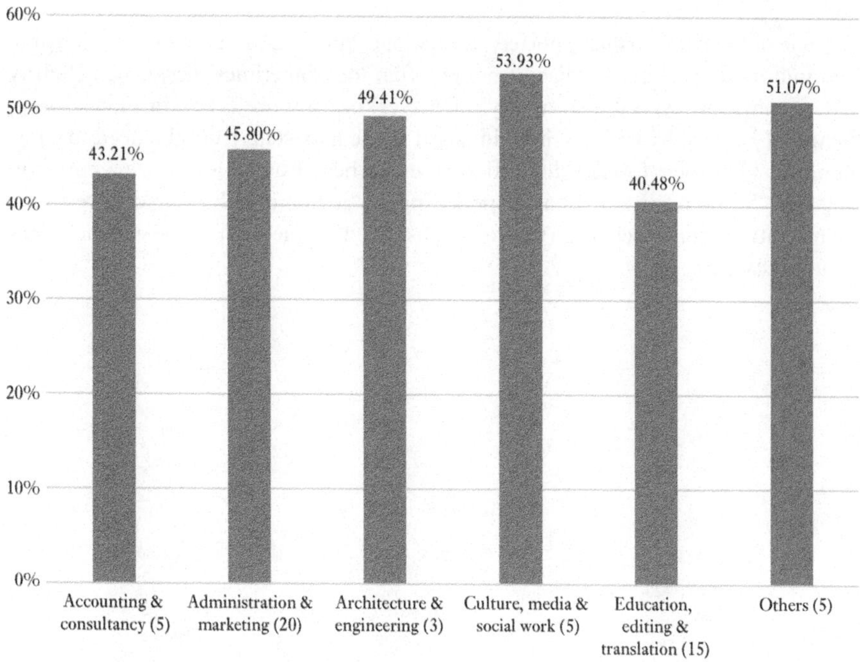

Figure 5.8 Comprehension and occupation

Comprehension and length of stay in an English-speaking country

Interestingly, the study findings reveal that participants who have never lived in an English-speaking country for a period of three months or more scored a slightly higher average comprehension rate of 26.21 marks out of a total of 56 (or 46.8%). This contrasts with the average comprehension rates of 42.26% and 44.32% attained respectively by those who reported having lived in an English-speaking country for three months to under a year and for a year or more (see Figure 5.9). A Pearson correlation analysis of the dataset shows a correlation coefficient of 0.02, suggesting a negligible correlation between the two variables in this case.

Comprehension and participants' use of English

As depicted in Figures 5.1 and 5.2 presented in this chapter, the majority of the participants reported infrequent use of English in their homes. Those who reportedly used English more often at home, at work and with friends were in general found to perform better than those who did so less frequently, as demonstrated in Figures 5.10 to 5.14.

None of the participants reported 'always' speaking English at home. Participants who indicated speaking English at home 'often' or 'sometimes' performed slightly better than those who did so 'rarely' or 'never' (see Figure 5.10). In Hong Kong, the use of English by Chinese individuals at home may stem from the need to communicate with their foreign domestic helpers, where English serves as a common language. Some parents may also speak English at home with their children who attend international schools, where English is the medium of instruction and communication.

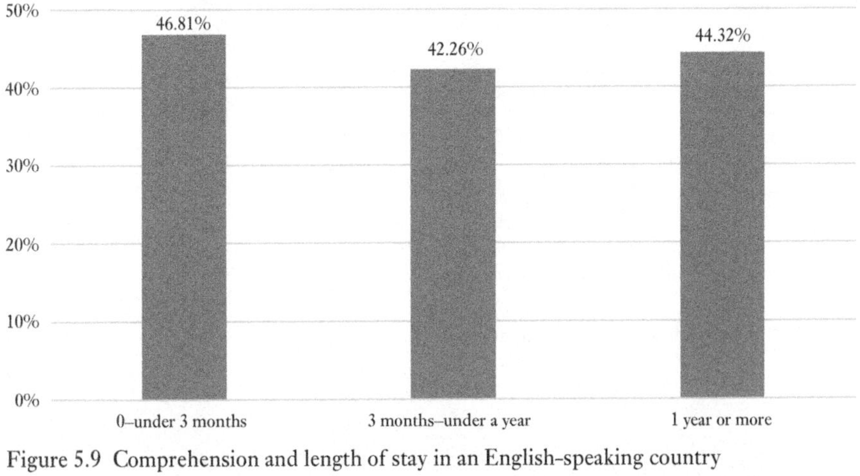

Figure 5.9 Comprehension and length of stay in an English-speaking country

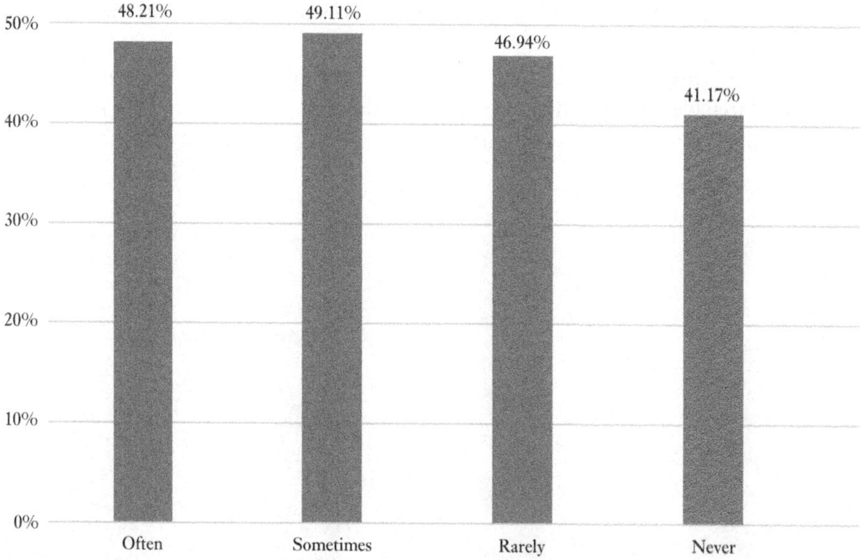

Figure 5.10 Comprehension and frequency of speaking English at home

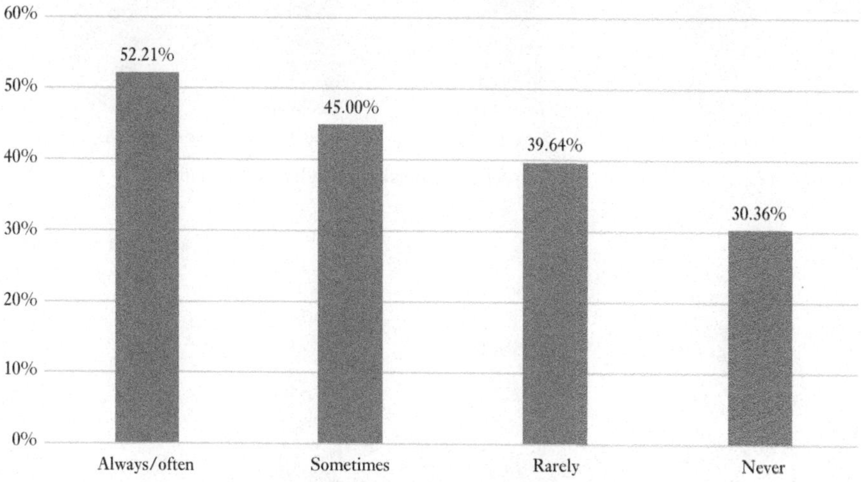

Figure 5.11 Comprehension and frequency of speaking English at work

Participants who reported speaking English at work more regularly (always/often) demonstrated significantly better comprehension of the courtroom discourse compared to those who only did so sometimes. Their performance was markedly superior to those who reported speaking English at work 'rarely' or 'never' (see Figure 5.11).

In a similar vein, among those who engaged in more frequent English conversations with their friends, a higher level of performance was observed compared to their counterparts who reported to 'rarely' or 'never' speak English with their friends (see Figure 5.12).

In terms of writing in English at work, those who reported to do so more often were found to have a slightly higher comprehension rate than their counterparts who only sometimes or rarely did so (Figure 5.13).

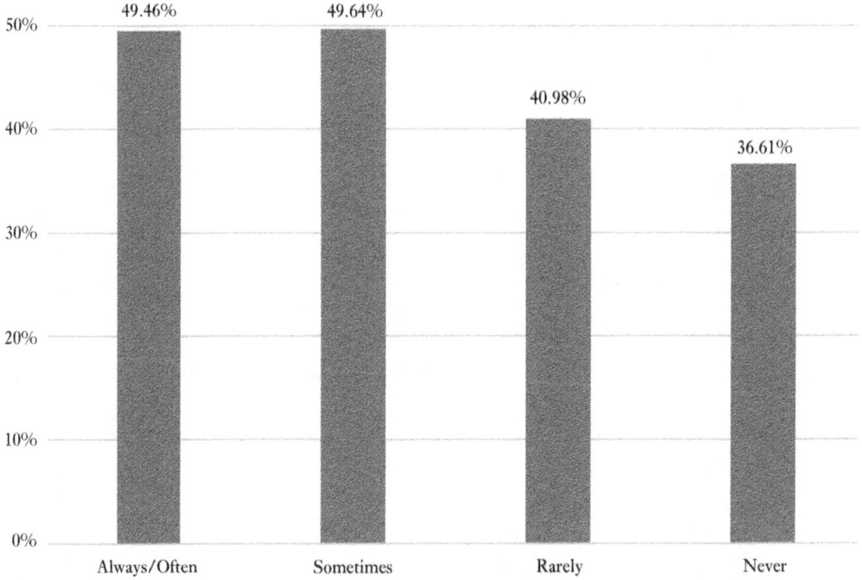

Figure 5.12 Comprehension and frequency of speaking English with friends

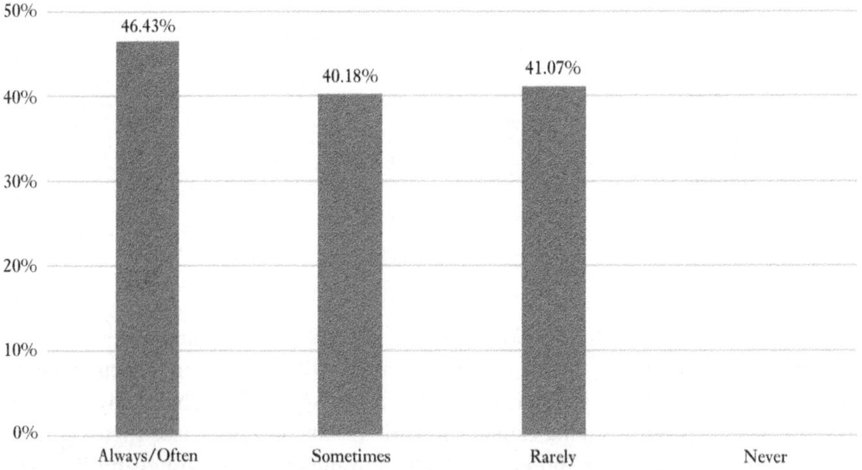

Figure 5.13 Comprehension and frequency of writing in English at work

The use of electronic messaging might explain why more participants reported writing in English when communicating with their friends (see Figure 5.2 earlier), albeit less frequently than writing in English at work. Typing in English for instant messaging is understandably faster than typing in Chinese. However, unlike the positive correlations observed above, a higher frequency in the use of English in this case was not found to be associated with a higher comprehension rate, as seen in Figure 5.14. Quite the contrary: those who purported to 'rarely' write in English when communicating with friends were found to have performed slightly better than those who did so 'sometimes' or 'regularly'. This is probably because communicating with friends in written English can be done in a casual manner and may be in 'Chinglish', which does not require as high a proficiency in English as writing in English at work.

Table 5.4 summarises the correlation coefficients of participants' usage of English at home, at work and when communicating with friends.

It can be noted from Table 5.4 that participants' use of spoken English has a positive correlation with their level of comprehension, with the strength of this

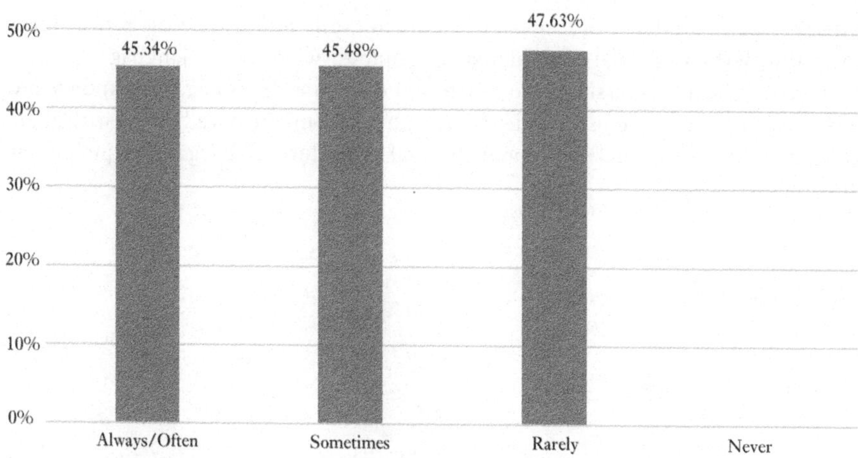

Figure 5.14 Comprehension and writing in English with friends

Table 5.4 Correlation coefficients between participants' comprehension and usage of English

Frequency	Correlation
Speaking English at home	0.253642776
Speaking English at work	0.293093143
Speaking English with friends	0.374730522
Writing in English at work	0.135770841
Writing in English for communicating with friends	−0.009253167

correlation ranging from very weak to weak. Participants' use of written English at work also demonstrates a positive but very weak correlation with their comprehension. The low correlation is possibly due to the fact that the need to use written English at work is commonplace in Hong Kong and does not necessarily equip participants with better listening comprehension skills. This is further suggested by the negative correlation of participants' comprehension levels and their use of written English for communicating with friends. As explained above, the need to use written English with friends most likely arises from the common use of instant messaging, which may not have any association with participants' English proficiency and listening comprehension skills.

Comprehension and jury experience

It is interesting to note from the results that those with actual jury experience in hearing cases in English had a comprehension level (43.21%) slightly lower than that of those without jury experience (45.42%), as illustrated in Figure 5.15. On the other hand, those with experience of serving in trials conducted in Chinese demonstrated a higher comprehension rate (53.57%). It stands to reason that those with previous experience of English trials did not fully understand the proceedings and those serving in trials conducted in Chinese, without the language barrier, were better able to understand the courtroom discourse. This cognitive knowledge gained from their previous experience in a jury trial might have helped with their understanding of the questions about the trial procedures and legal terminology in this study.

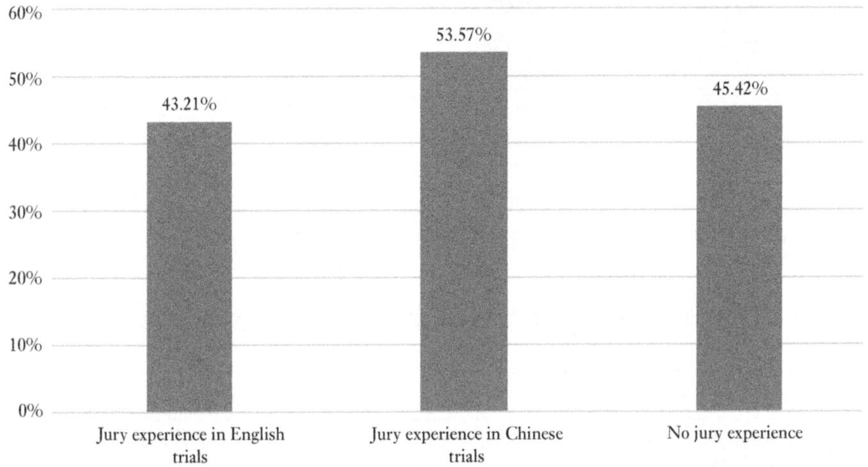

Figure 5.15 Comprehension and jury experience

Summary

This chapter has described the methodology of a study conducted to find out potential jurors' comprehension levels of courtroom discourse and presented its quantitative results. It also examined the association between participants' demographics and their scores in an attempt to identify potential correlations between their backgrounds and comprehension levels of the courtroom discourse. The results show that although there is a positive correlation between participants' comprehension and their education levels, the correlation is negligible. Surprisingly, participants with jury experience in English trials performed less well than those without jury experience. Participants with experience serving in Chinese trials outperformed both of these two groups, which is likely due to their familiarity with court proceedings and exposure to court language that contributed to understanding English courtroom discourse. It was also found that the experience of living in English-speaking countries does not seem to help with participants' comprehension. Without further information being obtained on this aspect such as the participants' exposure to English or frequency of speaking English during their stay overseas, it is hard to make any generalisation or conclusion from this finding. On the other hand, the results show that those who reported using spoken English more often at home, at work and when communicating with friends performed better than those who rarely or never had to do so. In comparison, frequent use of written English at work was found to correlate only weakly with participants' comprehension, and participants' use of written English for communicating with their friends had no positive correlation with their comprehension but a negative one of negligible magnitude.

In conclusion, the study has not revealed a strong correlation between participants' backgrounds and their comprehension levels. This can likely be attributed to the fact that potential jurors in Hong Kong predominantly share homogeneous backgrounds as a result of the education-level requirement, specifically being well educated and middle class. The next chapter will focus on the speakers and examine how speakers' voice projection, including their language style and speech animation, might be associated with participants' comprehension of the courtroom discourse.

Note

1. This study has gone through an ethics clearance process and received approval from the Human Research Ethics Committee (HREC) of the University of Hong Kong (HREC Reference No. E41611029).

6

Voice Projection and Jury Comprehension

The previous chapter described the conduct of my study, presented its results and examined correlations between participants' demographics and their levels of comprehension. The results of the study demonstrate that while some correlations, albeit weak, are easy to observe, such as participants' usage of spoken English and their levels of comprehension, others are negligible or statistically insignificant. This chapter uses Heffer's (2018) Voice Projection Framework as a conceptual tool to examine how speakers' voice projection might contribute to participants' listening comprehension problems.

Voice projection in courtroom discourse

As discussed in Chapter 3, voice projection involves projecting both physically and discursively (Heffer 2018). While physical voicing refers to the manner in which the message is animated, discursive voicing is the styling of the language used to articulate the message. Previous research on jury comprehension has primarily focused on discursive voicing and has largely overlooked the manner in which jury instructions are delivered – physical voicing in Heffer's (2018) terminology – and its impact on jurors' comprehension. The study detailed in this book set out to explore how physical voicing can be as important as discursive voicing to jurors' comprehension of courtroom discourse, especially for L2 jurors. The following section presents and categorises the problems identified by the participants as physical or discursive voicing problems and how these might have impacted on their understanding of the speech samples. The participants were provided with suggested factors, but they could choose more than one answer and provide additional free-form answers after hearing each speech segment.

Physical voicing and comprehension

Physical voicing involves the use of vocalics in articulating the verbal message; vocalics refer to vocal qualities such as pitch, volume, speaking rate and tone of voice that go along with the verbal message (Andersen 2008). Therefore, suggested options in my study questionnaire associated with physical voicing problems comprise factors such as speech rate, the speaker's accent, volume and articulation (which include stress, intonation and length of pauses). Table 6.1 illustrates the speakers' delivery rates, their accents and comprehension levels of the corresponding speech segments. The length of each speech segment is also included in the table. Only monologues were included in the analysis of speech rates and accents, with examination-in-chief and cross-examination of the witness excluded, as witness examination is dialogic in nature and involves two speakers. It would be impractical to measure the speech rates as counsel's questions and the witness's answers are sometimes too short for any meaningful comparison and correlation to be made. Transcripts of the speech segments used in my study are available in Appendix 2. Personal information in the transcripts and throughout this book has been redacted to ensure privacy.

Speech rate and comprehension

Table 6.1 presents the range of speakers' delivery rates, which vary from 86 to 208 words per minute (wpm). It appears that the slowest speech, delivered at a rate of 86 wpm, yields the highest comprehension rate of 82.48%. In contrast, the judge's summing-up in the murder case, delivered at a rate of 208 wpm, has a comprehension

Table 6.1 Speech rates, accents and comprehension

Discourse type	Accent[1]	Length of segment	No. of words	Speed (wpm)	Comprehension level
Murder					
Jury instructions	New Zealand	2m 6s	436	208	46.99%
Opening	Australian	4m 40s	596	128	42.07%
Examination-in-chief of witness	Australian and Chinese	1m 12s	251	N/A	15.09%
Cross-examination of witness	British and Chinese	3m 12s	434	N/A	33.96%
Summing-up	New Zealand	2m 14s	464	208	24.29%
Rape					
Jury instructions	British	3m 6s	353	114	31.60%
Opening	Chinese	4m 7s	353	86	82.48%
Summing-up	British	2m 37s	286	109	55.47%

rate of only 24.29%. However, it is worth noting that the jury instructions provided by the same judge in the same case, at the same rate of 208 wpm, demonstrates a higher comprehension rate of 46.99%. These findings suggest that other factors in addition to the speaking rate also influence speech comprehensibility.

Furthermore, a correlation test between the speech rates (in wpm) of the six speech segments and participants' comprehension levels yields a coefficient of –0.60. This strong negative correlation, falling within the range of 0.6 to 0.79 (Evans 1996) between the two variables, implies that higher speech rates are associated with lower comprehension levels. This correlation is supported by participants' responses, citing the judge's fast delivery rate in the murder trial as a significant obstacle to their comprehension, as depicted in Figure 6.1.

Figure 6.1 depicts a consolidated chart displaying the number of participants (out of a total of 53) who identified fast speech rate as a hindrance to their comprehension of the various speech segments. The chart reveals that the judge's rapid pace during both her instructions and summing-up to the jury in the murder trial was perceived by many participants as the most significant factor impeding their understanding. Note that the witness examination in the same case has been subdivided into counsel's questions and the witness's answers to account for the presence of two interlocutors with distinct accents and rates of speech. However, the rates of these speakers were not measured for the reasons explained earlier. In contrast to the murder trial judge, only a small number of participants reported speakers in the rape case as speaking too quickly, and no participants perceived the judge in his summing-up and the prosecutor in his opening address in the rape case to be speaking too fast. This is because these speakers in the rape case were, in fact, all speaking

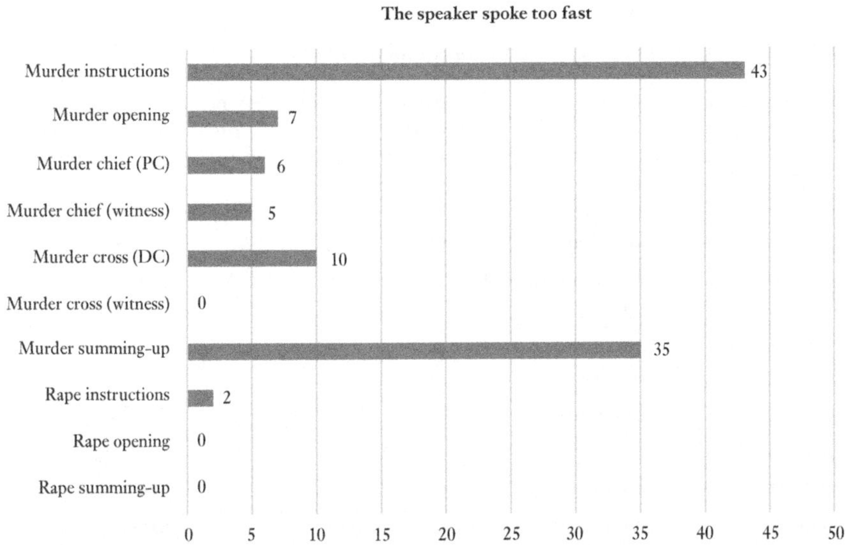

Figure 6.1 High speech rate perceived as an impeding factor

at a pace slower (or significantly slower) than the average oral reading rate of native English-speaking adults, reported to be between 150 and 180 wpm or 200 wpm in conversational speech (Calvert 1986: 178).

Speaker accent and comprehension

Regarding speaker accents, Table 6.1 indicates that the participants scored significantly lower on their comprehension when listening to native English speakers, but achieved a much higher comprehension level of 82.48% when listening to the Chinese-accented opening delivered by a local Chinese lawyer. This could be attributed to the fact that Chinese locals are accustomed to the typical Hong Kong accent commonly used by their teachers in primary and secondary schools, and possibly even in universities. One participant added a free-form comment, suggesting 'Gweilo accent' as a hindrance to comprehension.[2]

Figure 6.2 illustrates that a significant number of participants found the accent of the British defence counsel (DC) during the cross-examination of the witness in the murder trial to be the most challenging factor in their comprehension. This is followed by the New Zealand judge's instructions and summing-up, as well as the opening address of the Australian prosecution counsel (PC) in the same case. Interestingly, despite also being a 'Gweilo' accent, only seven and none of the participants consider the British accent of the judge in the rape case in his instructions and summing-up, respectively, to be a factor contributing to their comprehension difficulties. This discrepancy in perception could be ascribed to the latter judge's slow speech rate, along with his loud and clear articulation, and effective use of stress

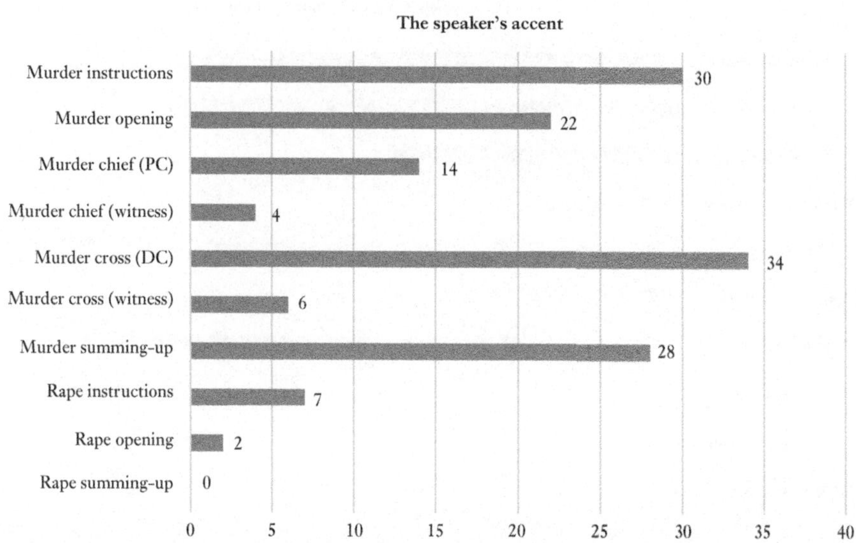

Figure 6.2 Speaker's accent perceived as an impeding factor

and intonation. These factors, which made his speech highly accessible to the audience, will be discussed below.

Speaker volume, articulation and comprehension

Perhaps there is not much the speakers could have done about their accents, which to a large extent are decided by their geographical origins and education. However, varying the manner of speaking could make a significant difference to listeners' comprehension of the voice being projected. Mumbling speech delivered at a low volume, and in a monotone with unchanging pitch and rhythm, is expected to adversely impact the comprehension of listeners. A study conducted by Keskin et al. (2019: 63) supports this notion, demonstrating that students' listening comprehension was adversely affected by a lack of prosodic variation in speech. Figures 6.3 and 6.4 present the results indicating that participants perceived the speakers' volumes and articulation as impeding their comprehension.

The differences in the results between the two trials as shown in Figure 6.3 are striking. Both the British judge and the Chinese prosecution counsel in the rape case were considered by the participants to be speaking loud enough for their comprehension. In the murder trial, however, both the judge and the DC were deemed to be speaking too softly. However, it must be noted that voice volume alone may not be the sole deciding factor. The clarity with which the message is articulated might be even more important for the message to be adequately understood. Figure 6.4 shows the numbers of participants who selected the option 'the speaker did not articulate clearly' as a comprehension-impeding factor.

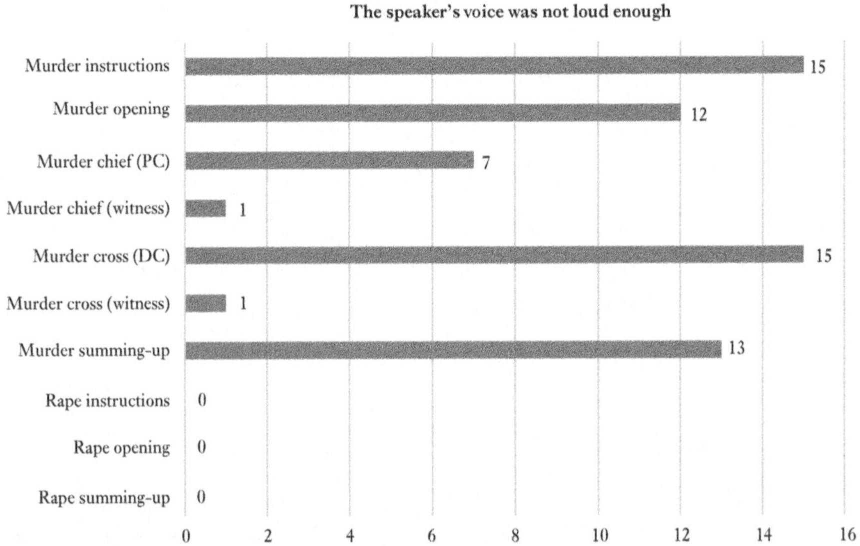

Figure 6.3 Speaker's soft voice perceived as an impeding factor

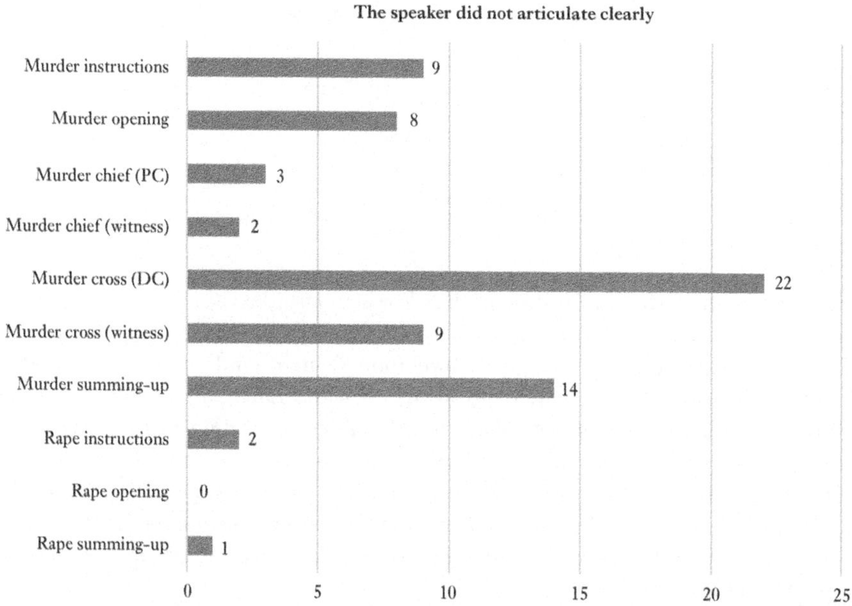

Figure 6.4 Speaker's poor articulation perceived as an impeding factor

Again, the differences between the two cases are substantial. In terms of the clarity of voice articulation, participants did not seem to experience any difficulty with speakers in the rape trial. The defence counsel in the murder case was again considered the least clear in his articulation, followed by the judge in the same case. As a matter of fact, both speakers delivered their speech in a monotonous manner, lacking the use of prosodic variation in stress and intonation to convey emphasis or captivate the audience. One participant commented on the defence counsel's manner of speaking in his cross-examination of the medical doctor in the murder trial, noting that 'the speaker was almost mumbling', his question 'is not clear enough' and he spoke 'without clear intonation'. Speaking of the New Zealand judge in her summing-up in the same case, one participant said 'that lady was close to mumbling', while another said 'she did not pause for the listeners' comprehension before proceeding to another point'.

In contrast, the speakers in the rape case, especially the judge, in addition to speaking slowly and at a high volume, were observed to have made use of frequent suprasegmental variation in animating their voice to reinforce the meaning of their message. To illustrate the use of stress, pauses and intonation versus the lack of variation of such suprasegmentals in the speakers' utterances, a comparison of the standard deviations in pitch range between the two judges' jury instructions and summing-up was made using Praat software (Boersma & Weenink 2022). Table 6.2 presents the standard deviations of the four speech segments.

Differences in the two judges' pitch ranges are enormous. Both the jury instructions and the summing-up in the murder case have much lower standard deviations

Table 6.2 Judges' pitch range standard deviations in the two trials

Speech segment	Pitch range standard deviation
Murder case jury instructions	33.51 Hz
Murder case summing-up	34.15 Hz
Rape case jury instructions	61.13 Hz
Rape case summing-up	63.61 Hz

than their counterparts in the rape trial. A low standard deviation in this case indicates that the judge's pitch stayed close to the mean, or in other words, the speech concerned was delivered at a relatively level tone. A high standard deviation, on the contrary, indicates that the pitch spread over a wider range, apparently resulting from the speaker's frequent use of rising and falling intonation in the utterances rather than a constant flat tone. A comparison of the waveforms and the pitch contours of the two judges in their summing-up, again generated using Praat analysis (Boersma & Weenink 2022), shows that there are far fewer pauses and other prosodic features including stress and intonation in the murder case summing-up than in that of the rape case.

To illustrate, a 10-second speech segment was extracted from each of the judges' summing-up, and their waveforms and pitch contours were compared. These are presented in Figures 6.5 and 6.6, along with extracts from transcripts of the corresponding speech segments (Extracts 6.1 and 6.2). In the transcript extracts, words in boldface indicate where stress is placed, whereas pauses are indicated in seconds in brackets; pauses of less than half a second are indicated with a dot. These transcription keys apply to all the transcripts used in this book (see Appendix 3 for the complete set of transcription keys used in this book).

Extract 6.1 (summing-up, murder case)

It's desired that you should all agree on your verdict but if you can't all agree, the court will accept verdicts of 6 to 1 (.) or 5 to 2, but there must be at least 5 of you who are agreed.

The relatively flat and closely clustered waveforms and pitch contours in Figure 6.5 indicate an almost constant amplitude and frequency – flat and monotonic speech delivered without much use of pauses or intonation.

On the contrary, the intermittent waveforms and pitch contours in Figure 6.6 illustrate the speaker's extensive use of pauses and prosodic variation (see also Extract 6.2).

Extract 6.2 (summing-up, rape case)

What then is rape?(1) A **man** commits **rape** (1) if **he** has (.) unlawful sexual intercourse (.) **with** a woman

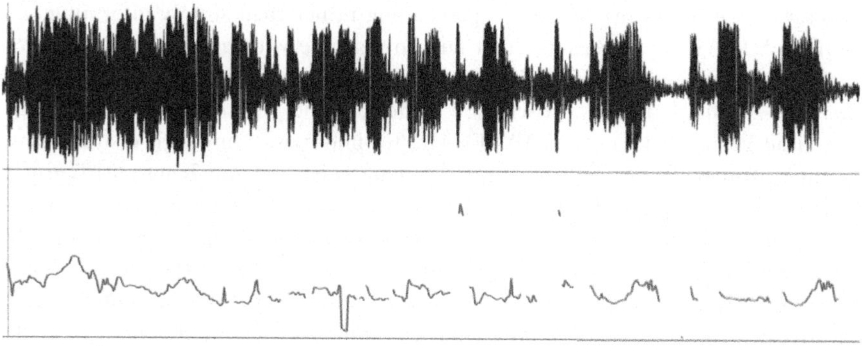

Figure 6.5 Waveform and pitch contour of Extract 6.1

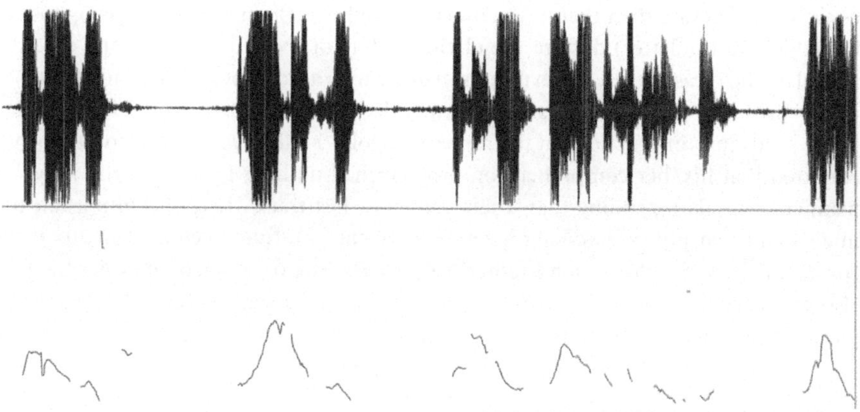

Figure 6.6 Waveform and pitch contour of Extract 6.2

The considerable difference between the two judges' speech rates is also evident in the lengths of Extracts 6.1 and 6.2, each of which has been transcribed from a 10-second speech segment. There are 41 words in the former but only 17 in the latter.

The discrete uses of prosodic features in the two speech segments are obvious, and the difference in the comprehension levels of the two speech segments is significant, one being 24.29% and the other 55.47%. Undeniably, a fast speech rate combined with poor articulation manifested in a lack of prosodic variation could have an adverse impact on the listeners' comprehension. Dumas (2000: 65) observes that 'instructions prepared to be read should not be delivered orally and rapidly in a monotone'. The monotony and rapidity in the speakers' delivery conveys a sense of disinterest and boredom, creating an impression that they are merely fulfilling their routine obligation of informing the listeners rather than genuinely connecting with the audience. Heffer (2018: 215) suggests that 'successful voice projection generally requires an orientation to persuading rather than simply informing the audience'. Inevitably, a message that fails to resonate with listeners will not persuade them. During the trial of George Zimmerman (*State of Florida* v. *George Zimmerman* [2012]), the key prosecution witness, Rachel Jeantel, testified in African American Vernacular English (AAVE). Her testimony was, however, dismissed by the jury as incomprehensible and unconvincing. Rickford and King (2016) argue that one reason for the dismissal of Jeantel's testimony has to do with her poor articulation, manifested in her underbite, low pitch and soft speaking. This made it challenging for listeners to comprehend an unfamiliar dialect (Rickford & King 2016: 965–976). Similarly, Cantonese-speaking jurors may struggle to understand courtroom speech delivered in an accent with which they are unfamiliar, particularly when spoken in a low, mumbling monotone that fails to engage and thus persuade them.

It must, however, be noted that the jury instructions in the rape case had a lower comprehension rate than that in the murder case (31.60% in the former as opposed to 46.99% in the latter) despite the obvious effort of the judge in the rape case to articulate the message in a much clearer manner with a slow speech rate and frequent use of prosodic variation. This is confirmed by one participant who said that the judge in his jury instructions in the rape case spoke 'really clearly'. This participant admitted that his/her comprehension problem had nothing to do with the judge's manner of speaking, adding that 'I just somehow lost track'. It is thus important to understand that physical voicing is only one of the two fundamental elements that constitute the Voice Projection Framework. Successful projection of the voice hinges also on discursive voicing, that is, the actual language used, not only the paralanguage. This will be examined and discussed below.

Discursive voicing and comprehension

While animating 'is physically conveying voice through sound, sign and other forms of semiosis', styling means 'the selecting and arranging of words, sentences, paragraphs and so on' (Heffer 2018: 212). This section presents the results of factors relating to discursive voicing perceived by the participants as contributing to their comprehension difficulties. Examples are cited from their answers and from the transcripts to illustrate the styling problem of the language used by the speakers. Discursive projection of the voice is primarily reflected in the diction or terminology and the syntax of the language used. In other words, of the two suggested factors, one relates to the presence of technical terms and the concepts behind, and the other is the use of lengthy sentences. As discussed in Chapter 3, studies on jury comprehension in English-dominant common law courtrooms have all pointed to the use of legal language in jury instructions as the primary source of jury comprehension problems. In the case of L2 jurors, comprehension problems might arise not only from the use of legal language, as plain language might also prove challenging for them, as discussed in Chapter 5. This section will present the typical linguistic features of courtroom language indicated by the participants as impeding their comprehension, while their comprehension of non-technical language will be examined in the subsequent section.

Medical and legal terms

Figure 6.7 shows the number of participants who perceived terminology to be an impeding factor in their comprehension of the various speech segments. It illustrates that the examination of the medical doctor, both examination-in-chief and cross-examination, contains the most technical terms, obviously because the doctor's evidence mentioned numerous medical terms relating to the treatment he provided to the victim before his death. Likewise, technical terminology in the jury instructions of both cases and in the judge's summing-up of the murder case was found by the participants to have impeded their comprehension.

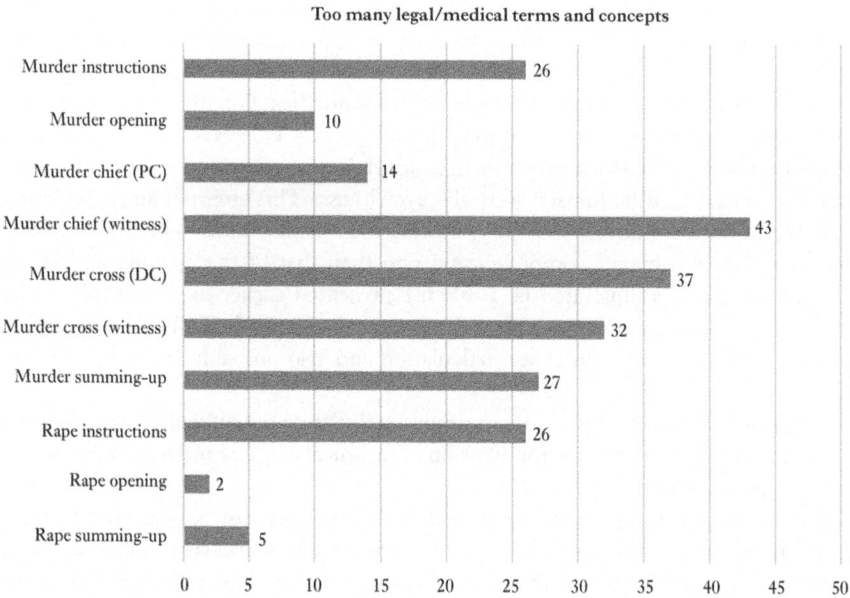

Figure 6.7 Legal/medical terminology perceived as an impeding factor

In contrast, the opening addresses of both counsel were considered the least problematic as they related to the facts of the cases rather than the law, and thus the language used was the least legalistic. This is illustrated in Extracts 6.3 and 6.4.

Extract 6.3 Opening speech (murder case)

And Madam [redacted] will tell you that she saw the accused go to the kitchen of the premises (1) and pick up (1) a chopper, an item which is common enough in Hong Kong, and you've all seen them before. She will tell you that the accused came out of the kitchen with the chopper, uh on seeing this, she will tell you that, her ex-husband tried to leave the premises, uh, he exited. And she will tell you that he was chased (.) by the accused, armed with the chopper down the stairs leading from the third floor to the ground floor.

Extract 6.4 Opening address (rape case)

After Ms [redacted] had lain down for a while, the accused climbed onto the ladder that was beside the bed, and started chatting with her again. Then at some point, the accused started to kiss Ms [redacted] by force, and against her will. Ms [redacted] attempted to resist his advances by saying no and pushing him away. However, she failed in her attempts to push him away. The accused eventually climbed onto the bed, took off Ms [redacted]'s clothing, and had sexual intercourse with her against her will.

In Extracts 6.3 and 6.4, both counsel were giving the jury a preview about what the witnesses would be telling the court. In both cases, plain language was used without technical vocabulary. In Extract 6.3, the prosecution counsel made it clear to the jury that he was simply relaying what the eyewitness would be telling the court by specifying the source of the information, using reported speech. However, in Extract 6.4, the prosecution counsel assumed the role of a storyteller or a narrator without mentioning the witness, as if he himself were the eyewitness. This storytelling presentation style might have appealed to the jury, making the opening address highly accessible and resulting in a higher comprehension rate than that of the opening address in the murder case, as illustrated in Table 6.1 presented earlier in this chapter. The comprehension rate might have been further enhanced by the Chinese prosecution counsel's slow speaking rate, clear articulation and also probably his familiar Hong Kong accent.

The rest of this section provides examples to illustrate the difficulties encountered by the participants in their comprehension of technical medical and legal terms in the various speech segments.

By way of background, the defendant in the murder case was alleged to have killed the husband of his landlady with a chopper (Chinese cleaver) when the victim accompanied his wife to visit the premises in question to demand outstanding rent from the defendant. The defence case was that the defendant acted in self-defence and thus should be charged with manslaughter instead. The defence further argued that medical maltreatment led to the death of the victim and that the two blows administered to the victim's head by the defendant were not fatal, and therefore the jury might even consider a verdict for wounding.

One of the prosecution witnesses, a medical doctor who treated the victim in hospital, told the court in his testimony-in-chief that he tried to stop the bleeding by suturing the laceration wound on the victim's scalp. The defence counsel (DC) in his cross-examination of the witness, however, suggested that the suturing of the scalp was undesirable as it would result in further bleeding inside the brain, that is, subdural haemorrhage. Extract 6.5 illustrates the language used by the DC in his cross-examination of the witness, who struggled to understand and reply to him. Note that the Chinese witness, despite opting to testify in English without the assistance of an interpreter, appeared to lack the necessary English proficiency to comprehend the DC's questions or to express himself adequately and accurately. This led to noticeable communication issues between the DC and the witness, possibly rendering it even more difficult for the jurors to understand the testimony. The challenges facing Chinese witnesses who testify in English and the resultant impact on the communication process are explored in detail in Ng (2020).

Extract 6.5 Cross-examination of witness (murder case)

DC: If your suturing is highly effective, one hundred per cent effective, but nevertheless below it, some further bleeding or pressure develops, if it can't es—if that pressure can't escape through the suture holes, the pressure would be applied to the brain.

W: (2) Mmm. (1) An::d (2) actually we e:::r (.) actually I— (.) I er (2) I'm sorry, can you (.) can you=

DC: =Well, in this case we hear that, eventually, when the head was opened up at some time after six a.m., the pressure was such that the brain was displaced slightly to one side.

W: Yes.

DC: Right? What I'm saying is that er, if there was no drain and the sutures were totally effective, any further development of pressure (.) beneath the sutures would have nowhere to escape.

W: (6) Actually the su— the:: (.) the scalp was sutured in the full thickness, and the:: the— the— the bleeding was er (.) e::r (.) was stopped by that, so e:: r (.) you mean er (2) and (2.5) and e::r (2) actually I'm— I'm quite— I'm not quite understand your question. Can you er (.) er repeat it again?

....

DC: All I'm saying is that, had the subdural haemorrhage been dealt with surgically (.) much earlier on, this patient would have stood a much better chance of survival.

When asked to explain a 'laceration wound' (Question B30 in the questionnaire) and 'suturing' (Question B37), only 22.64% and 15.09% of the participants were able to do so, respectively, and fewer (13.21%) were able to explain what 'subdural haemorrhage' was (Question B38). One participant had this to say: 'I am not sure what they were talking about. Only know that they were discussing something over the victim's brain.'

Legal terms were found to be equally, if not more, problematic. When asked to explain the meaning of 'verdict' (Question B3), some participants took it to mean 'suspect', 'defendant', 'the convicted person' or even 'the murderer'; others associated it with the meaning of 'offence', 'jury', 'evidence' or even 'ratio'.

When explaining the verdicts to the jury in her summing-up, the judge in the murder trial said that 'it's desired that you should all agree on your verdict', as cited in Extract 6.1 above. Only 4 out of the 53 participants (or 7.55%) answered the question 'What would be a verdict preferred by the court?' (Question B43) correctly.

With regard to the alternative offence to murder of which the defendant might be convicted if the jury found him not guilty of murder, the judge gave the following explanation (Extract 6.6):

Extract 6.6 Summing-up (murder case)

So you've got one relating to the count of murder, one relating to the alternative count of manslaughter. And you will be asked on what basis you deliver your verdict of manslaughter or whether it is on a basis of unlawful act, or whether it is on the basis of provocation.

In relation to this extract, two questions were asked. One is 'What is the alternative count of offence to murder the defendant may be convicted of?' (Question B46); the other is 'If the defendant is convicted of this alternative offence, on which two bases can this offence be?' (Question B47). Only 10 participants out of the total 53 (or 18.87%) provided a correct answer to the first question, and none of them answered the second question correctly.

In the rape trial, the complainant was a lesbian who used to live in the same flat with the defendant when she was a girlfriend of the defendant's younger sister. On the day in question, the complainant, having broken up with the defendant's younger sister, returned to the flat to collect her belongings when the defendant was alone in the premises. The defendant subsequently had sexual intercourse with the complainant, allegedly against her will.

In his instructions to the jury, the judge explained the system of justice in Hong Kong in this way (Extract 6.7):

Extract 6.7 Jury instructions (rape case)

The system of justice which we practise is adversarial in nature, which means that the presentation and examination of witnesses is substantially in control of counsel for prosecution and counsel for the defence.

None of the participants provided the correct answer to the question 'What is the word used by the judge to describe the system of justice practised in Hong Kong?' (Question B53). The word 'adversarial' was perhaps alien to them, or they simply failed to hear it.

The judge went on to explain the two fundamental principles in the common law adversarial system (Extract 6.8):

Extract 6.8 Jury instructions (rape case)

Now, throughout the trial you must keep in mind two very important principles of the, the Hong Kong system of criminal law and justice. These are

> **fundamental** to the trial. The **first** of these is that the prosecution must prove the accused's guilt. **He does not** have to prove his (.) innocence. The second of this is that before you may convict the accused, you must be satisfied beyond (.) reasonable doubt that he is guilty. That is the same thing as being sure of his guilt. Nothing less than that will do.

With reference to this remark, the participants were first asked to name the two important principles in the criminal justice system of Hong Kong (Question B55), and 19 (or 35.85%) of them answered this question correctly. When asked to explain what 'being satisfied beyond reasonable doubt' about the defendant's guilt means (Question B56), only 14 (or 26.42%) of the participants were able give a correct answer. Incorrect answers included 'the benefit of doubt goes to the defendant' and 'make a fair conclusion'.

In his summing-up to the jury, the judge highlighted the three important elements required for the jury to convict the defendant of rape, namely 1) the defendant had sexual intercourse with the complainant, 2) the complainant did not consent to it, and 3) the defendant either knew that the complainant did not consent or he 'was reckless as to whether she consented'.

When asked to explain what 'reckless' means (Question B72), only 14 (or 26.42%) of the participants provided a correct answer. Many simply said they were not sure or did not know the meaning, while some took it to mean 'ruthless', 'shameless' 'forcible' or 'rude'.

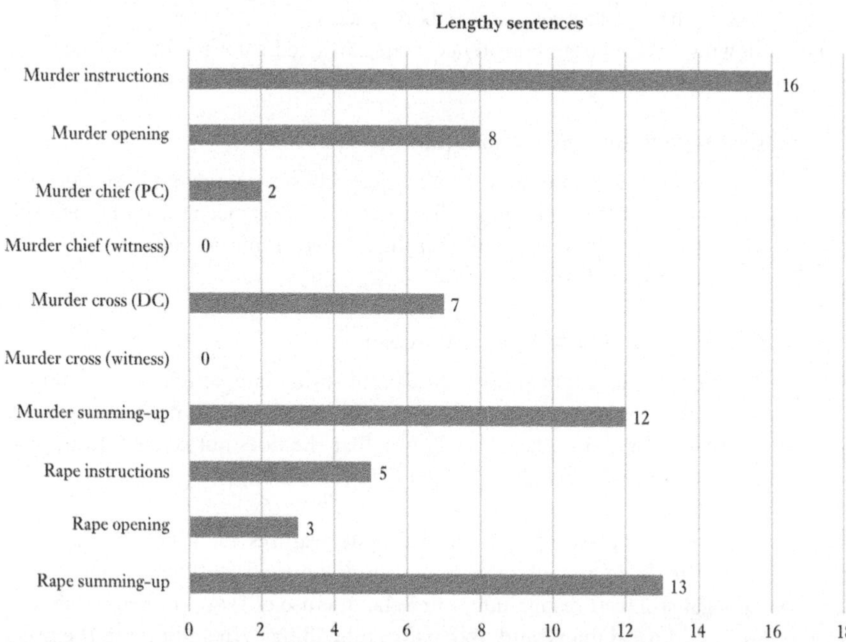

Figure 6.8 Lengthy sentences perceived as an impeding factor

Lengthy sentences

In comparison, lengthy syntactic structures of the language used were found to be less of a problem than technical terminology. Figure 6.8 shows that long sentences were perceived as a problem primarily in the jury instructions in the murder case, followed by the judge's summing-up in the rape case. Table 6.3 compares the average sentence lengths of all the monologues in the two cases.

Table 6.3 Average sentence lengths of monologues

Monologue	**Average sentence length (in no. of words)**
Murder case jury instructions	20.8
Murder case opening	17.5
Murder case summing-up	23.2
Rape case jury instructions	20.8
Rape case opening	18.6
Rape case summing-up	23.8

The general perception of the participants is consistent with the statistics in Table 6.3. As expected, the opening addresses of both counsels have shorter sentences as they are of a narrative genre – thus the least legalistic in nature – and were delivered primarily in plain English, as mentioned above. In comparison, the jury instructions and summing-up have longer sentences in both cases.

The following are two typical sentences, one extracted from the jury instructions in the murder case and the other from the summing-up in the rape case.

> **Extract 6.9** Jury instructions (murder case)
>
> Now, members of the jury, you've been chosen as jurors to consider the facts of this case and eventually to return a verdict as to whether this defendant is guilty or not guilty of the offence of murder with which he has been charged. (44 words)

> **Extract 6.10** Summing-up (rape case)
>
> A man commits a rape if he has unlawful sexual intercourse with a woman, who at that the time does not consent to it, and if, at the time he has sexually intercourse with her, he either knows that she does not consent to it, or is reckless as to whether she consents to it. (55 words)

The two sentences display some of the legalistic features identified by Charrow and Charrow (1979) as impeding jurors' comprehension in their experimental study. Such legalistic features include, inter alia, the use of 'as to' in lieu of 'about', 'technical or legal lexical items' and 'too many embeddings'. In addition to the presence of legal terms, which has been discussed above, both sentences use 'as to' in 'as to whether' and each has multiple embeddings with a cluster of dependent and independent clauses, especially in the second extract; and both are compound and complex sentences, which could have been split into several simple sentences to enhance jurors' comprehension.

The use of legal terminology (along with occasional medical terminology in the murder case) and lengthy complex sentence structures have likely contributed to listeners' comprehension problems. When asked about what contributed to their comprehension problem with the jury instructions in the murder case, one participant said, 'The judge did not speak in plain language', while others expressed difficulties in understanding legal terms used in the judges' speeches and medical terms in the witness examination.

Other perceived impeding factors

In addition to problems arising from the physical and discursive voice projection of the speakers, other problems identified by the participants as hindering their comprehension will be discussed below.

Background noise

One inevitable source of background noise in both cases is the *chuchotage* provided by the interpreter, which as discussed in Chapter 4 is usually audible only to the defendant in the dock but may sound like an indistinct murmur to other people in court. This simultaneous whispering is also picked up by the digital recording system. However, how distracting this murmur is to jurors or other participants in court listening to the original English speech might depend on the manner in which the speech is delivered. This will be discussed later in this section. The murder case also has another source of noise – the typing sound of the judge, who invariably produced this noise by typing to take notes of other speakers' utterances. As the judge explained in the other part of her jury instructions (which was not included in the recording for my study), she kept comprehensive running notes for quick checks when necessary during the trial.

As shown in Figure 6.9, background noise was indicated as more of a problem in the murder trial than in the rape trial, especially in the PC's opening address and in the DC's cross-examination of the witness, largely due to the key striking sound produced by the judge during the process of typing. One participant made this comment: 'The typing sound is quite annoying and I can't concentrate on listening', while another said 'the typing sound makes me nervous'.

The judge's own speeches (instructions and summing-up to the jury) also recorded relatively high numbers of participants indicating background noise as an impeding factor despite the fact that there was no typing sound. Obviously the judge could not and did not need to type concurrently when she herself was speaking. The primary source of the background noise in the judge's instructions and summing-up in the murder trial and in other speakers' speeches in the rape case is

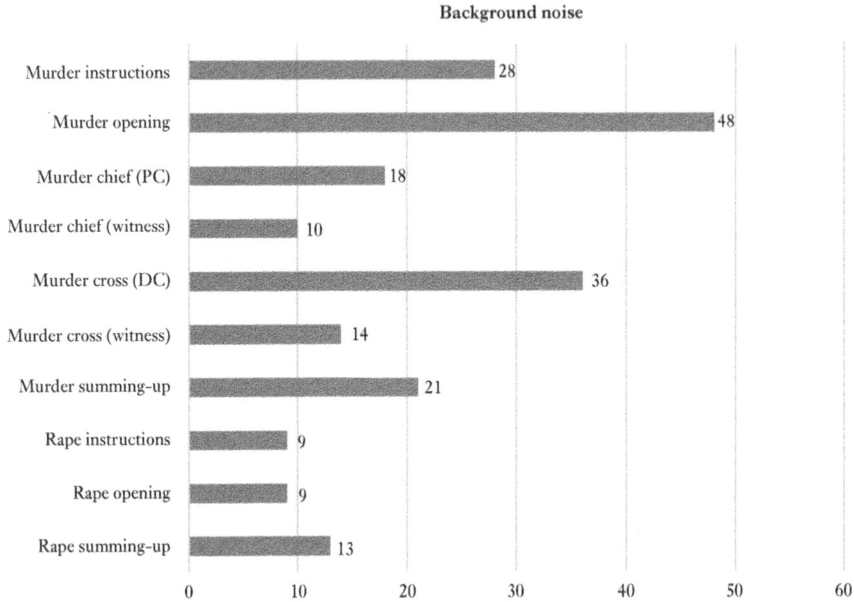

Figure 6.9 Background noise perceived as an impeding factor

the interpreter's *chuchotage*. While not all judges type to take notes, thus producing an interfering sound to the listeners, the *chuchotage* of the interpreter is almost unavoidable in trials conducted in English. This is due to the need to interpret for the defendant (mostly Cantonese-speaking in the context of Hong Kong) in the dock, as explained in Chapter 4. The reason why the interpreter's *chuchotage* seems to have bothered the listeners more in the judge's speech in the murder trial than in that of the other speakers in the rape case might have to do with the way the speakers animated their voices. If a speaker talks in a more 'lively' and thus engaging tone with the use of stress and intonation, at an adequate volume and a slow pace, this may mitigate the impact of the background noise on the listeners. Conversely, if the speech is delivered with a level tone, at a low volume and a fast pace as the judge in the murder case did, the background noise would become more audible and thus distracting to the listeners.

Lack of visual cues and background information

Other reasons for the listening comprehension problem suggested by the participants include not being able to benefit from face-to-face communication; as one participant said, 'when you can't see the face and mouth movement of the speaker, it would be harder to understand a foreign language'. Another had this to say: 'we can only hear the sound; if we are in the court, we can gain better understanding by seeing the lawyers, defendant in person, and that will help our understanding'.

This suggests that for L2 listeners' comprehension, non-verbal communication such as being able to see the speaker' facial expressions and lip movements is important. One participant noted that in court, jurors might be able to see some pictures and that would help their understanding. Indeed, the lack of visual cues might have had an impact on the participants' comprehension of the courtroom discourse, especially for L2 listeners.

A couple of other participants mentioned the absence of background information about the trials as another factor impeding their comprehension. As a matter of fact, participants were provided with the statement of offence for each case on the questionnaire, the kind of information jurors are provided on the indictment they are given. An indictment usually also contains a list of witnesses of the case, as explained by the prosecution counsel in his opening address to the jury. However, the information about the witnesses is not relevant in this case, and therefore its omission presumably would not have had any impact on the participants' comprehension. A brief introduction about each recording was also provided on the questionnaire telling the participants the kind of speech they were going to hear. For example, before the recording of the witness's examination-in-chief in the murder case, this is what they saw on the questionnaire: 'You are about to hear the examination-in-chief of an expert witness, a medical doctor who provided treatment to the victim in the hospital.'

Participants' self-admission of inadequacy in English proficiency and other problems

Other participants attributed the listening comprehension problem to their own insufficiency in English proficiency or lack of concentration. A few of them said '[it's due to] my listening ability' or 'I lack confidence in English listening', while another admitted 'my vocab is weak'. Another participant raised the stress and tension of being a first-time juror and being psychologically unprepared as a reason for the comprehension problem, adding that the comprehension problem might exist even if the trial was conducted in Cantonese. Potential jurors' comprehension of trials conducted in Cantonese is an interesting topic which warrants further investigation but is beyond the scope of the present study.

Comprehension of non-technical terms

While most of the questions concerning legal or medical terms and trial procedures were poorly answered, comprehension problems were, however, not restricted to technical terminology or legal procedures; non-technical terms related to the facts of the case were also found to pose challenges to the potential jurors' comprehension. Extract 6.11 has been excerpted from the prosecution's opening address, where the prosecution counsel was telling the jury what the witness saw when she reached the ground floor:

Extract 6.11 Opening address (murder case)

> She didn't actually see them going down the stairs. By the time she got to the ground floor, she could see her ex-husband and the defendant grappling over the chopper. And she will tell you that there was clearly uh a chop wound on the uh her ex-husband' head and he was bleeding profusely.

In relation to this, a question (B23) was asked: 'Did Madam [redacted] see the defendant attack the victim?' Only 23 respondents got the correct negative answer, with an accuracy rate of 43.40% – 16 selected 'Yes', while 14 chose 'Not sure' as their answer.

In Extract 6.12, taken from the summing-up of the murder trial, the judge was explaining to the jury the procedure of delivering the verdict in court after the jury's deliberations and return to the courtroom.

Extract 6.12 Summing-up (murder case)

> I will explain what will happen when you come back to court. Mr Foreman will be asked to stand up and then the clerk will ask (.) the questions for the charges as set out on those forms.

In relation to this, the participants were asked this question (B49): 'When the jury comes back to the court, who will ask the jury foreman questions in relation to the charge?' Only 9 out of the total 53 participants (16.98%) selected the correct answer out of the four options provided. There is no reason to believe that the participants had a problem understanding the word 'clerk'. Their comprehension problem is more likely to do with the speaker's physical voicing of the message that failed to carry to her audience.

As noted earlier in this chapter, the prosecutor's opening address in the rape case yielded the highest score, presumably due to his comprehension-friendly manner of articulation and the narrative genre of the speech. Nonetheless, the occasional use of a formal term was also found to pose comprehension problems for the participants. Extract 6.13 is an example of this, where the prosecutor in the rape trial was telling the jury what the victim did when she was not able to gain entry to the apartment on the day in question.

Extract 6.13 Opening address (rape case)

> Initially, she could not get in, as she no longer had the keys to the premises. She waited for about two hours in the vicinity of the premises.

The use of the prepositional phrase 'in the vicinity of' instead of a more common preposition 'near' was apparently found to be less comprehensible by the participants, as only 19 (35.85%) of them correctly answered the question (B62) 'Where did the victim wait for Ms [redacted] to come back?'

While a wrong answer to some of the questions cited above might not be critical to jurors' comprehension of the entire proceedings and thus to the final verdict, a wrong answer to certain questions such as Question B23 cited earlier, which suggests miscomprehension of the eyewitness's evidence, could be significant and might result in an entirely different outcome of the trial.

A legal expert's perspective

In order to have an external opinion of the courtroom discourse of the two trials, a legal expert was invited to listen to the recordings and to answer the questions in Sections B and C. This was followed by a brief interview to solicit her comments on the courtroom discourse used in the two trials, focusing on the recording (Section B). The legal expert is a barrister-at-law and an experienced trainer in trial advocacy at the Faculty of Law in my home university. She had been practising law for 22 years at the time of the study, was born in Hong Kong, Indian by ethnicity and speaks English as her first language.

She likewise found the physical voicing of the speakers in the murder case, especially that of the judge and the defence counsel, problematic. She said the judge in the murder case spoke with a 'strong New Zealand accent' and 'very quickly', and that she 'mumbled' and her 'sentences ran into each other' without pauses in her jury instructions. She also pointed out that the judge sounded rushed, bored and disinterested in her summing-up to the jury. Her comment on the defence counsel in his cross-examination of the witness was that he 'mumbled' and was 'not clear' in his articulation.

On the other hand, she commended the judge and the prosecutor in the rape case for articulating their messages so clearly and slowly, which in her opinion was conducive to the comprehension of the listeners, especially listeners without a native command of the English language.

The use of legal terminology without explanation was seen as another problem that might hinder the participants' comprehension of the discourse, even when delivered with a clear articulation. For example, she noted that the prosecutor in the murder case did not explain what an indictment was in his opening address, and that the judge in the rape case did not explain the meaning of 'reckless'.

As a native English speaker with a legal background, she was able to answer most of the questions correctly, with the exception of a couple of questions about the facts, where she admitted that she had lost track or could not hear the speaker clearly. She added, however, that she was able to answer most of the questions because of her legal background and her native command of the English language.

In a similar vein, she found the typing sound of the judge in the murder trial distracting. However, she did not make any note of the Cantonese *chuchotage* of the interpreter in both cases or flag that as a problem, probably because she has only limited proficiency in Cantonese and therefore did not find the Cantonese whispering distracting.

The legal expert agreed with some listeners that the absence of visual cues associated with the use of audio recording might have disadvantaged the listeners. However, she remarked at the same time that listening to the audio recordings in a language lab with headphones might actually have mitigated the disadvantage of not being able to see the facial cues of the speakers. She pointed out that speakers' voices might not be clearly heard in court due to the physical distance between where they speak and the jury box. She added that there are other sources of distraction that might arise in an actual courtroom setting, where people are free to move around, or enter and exit the courtroom. She concluded that it was the use of technical terms, legal and medical included, as well as the speakers' manner of speaking, that made their speech difficult to understand, particularly for L2 listeners.

Summary

This chapter has examined and discussed how the physical and discursive voice projection of the courtroom discourse may have influenced the understanding of the participants. The findings of my study show that, while legalese and technical evidence are to blame for the participants' comprehension problems, poorly articulated speech was equally, if not more, challenging to L2 jurors' comprehension. It can be argued that the manner in which a message is delivered is expected to impact listeners' comprehension in general, yet L2 speakers may be more susceptible to poorly articulated messages due to their lack of proficiency in the language. In particular, speakers' delivery rate is found to have a strong negative correlation with listeners' comprehension. Findings of the comprehension test demonstrate that L2 jurors' comprehension problems are not limited to legalese or technical terminology. Plain and ordinary English may also be incomprehensible to the listeners if the speakers do not articulate the message clearly and slowly. Some participants attributed their comprehension problems to their lack of proficiency in the English language or to the background noise. The chapter has also included insights and feedback from a legal expert about the use of legal language and the speakers' manner of speaking, which further validate the findings and observations of this study. The next chapter will explore the feasibility of providing interpretation services for jurors as a means to alleviate the linguistic disadvantage experienced by L2 jurors and promote equal participation in jury service, with a focus on juries in Hong Kong.

Notes

1. A British barrister-at-law invited to listen to the recordings confirmed the accents of the expatriate speakers as such. She recognised the voices of some of the legal personnel in the two trials.
2. Gweilo is a Cantonese transliteration for foreigners or expatriates.

7

Interpreting for Jurors

In light of the findings presented in the previous two chapters, this chapter explores the use of interpreters to assist in jury comprehension, which has the benefit of promoting equal participation and thus upholding the principle of trial by jury. This chapter surveys the provision of sign language interpreting for deaf jurors in common law jurisdictions and argues for NES/LEP individuals to be treated equally in their right to participate in jury service. It also draws on the successful experience of New Mexico, which allows NES/LEP jurors to sit in trials with the assistance from interpreters. This chapter argues for the same service to be provided for jurors in Hong Kong, which shares a comparable linguistic landscape with New Mexico. Furthermore, this chapter addresses general concerns regarding jurors' access to interpreter-mediated discourse. In particular, it examines conflicting judicial opinions of two appellate courts in Hong Kong concerning an appeal related to jurors' access to interpreted courtroom discourse, and discusses the implications and challenges for the longstanding standard practice of court interpreting in Hong Kong.[1]

Interpreting for defendants in the legal process

As noted in Chapter 1, one of the key safeguards of the right to a fair trial, as specified in the International Covenant on Civil and Political Rights (ICCPR) (United Nations 1966), is the provision of free interpreting services for defendants who do not speak the language used in criminal proceedings. Interpreting is therefore by and large a standard service provided for defendants facing criminal charges in ICCPR-compliant jurisdictions. This is to ensure defendants' effective participation in the judicial process, and thus to avoid compromising their right to a fair trial. In Hong Kong, as noted in Chapter 4, from the very beginning of the British colonial rule to the present post-colonial time, interpreters have long played an indispensable role in the judicial process because of the use of English as a trial language in a predominantly Cantonese-speaking Chinese society.

Interpreting for jurors

However, interpreting for jurors, who determine defendants' guilt or innocence in jury trials, is a rarity because individuals are generally not eligible to serve on juries if they are unable to understand the language used in court proceedings, as explained in Chapter 2. Interpreting for jurors, if any, has hitherto been limited to sign language interpreting with a view to enabling deaf people's civil right to serve on juries and to eliminate discrimination. The following section examines common law jurisdictions which allow deaf persons to participate in jury service through the assistance of sign language interpreters and reviews relevant studies.

Interpreting for deaf jurors

In the United States, the Rehabilitation Act of 1973 and the Americans with Disabilities Act (ADA) of 1990 have been employed to facilitate the full participation of deaf people on juries with the assistance of sign language interpreters throughout the courts in the country (Boyle 2011; Gonzales Rose 2011, 2014, 2020; Johnson 2016). In some states, deaf people have been performing the civic duty as jurors since 1979, assisted by sign language interpreters who, like all jurors, swear an oath to maintain the confidentiality of jury deliberations (Napier & McEwin 2015; Napier et. al. 2018).

In New Zealand, blind or deaf individuals are permitted to serve on juries as the Juries Act 1981 does not include physical capacity as a criterion for disqualification from jury service (Boyle 2011; Napier & McEwin 2015). The first deaf person was empanelled in 2005 in New Zealand as a juror and even elected as the jury foreman, assisted by sign language interpreters throughout the trial and jury deliberations (Napier & McEwin 2015; Napier et. al. 2018).

Like the United States and New Zealand, Canada has allowed deaf persons to serve as jurors since 1998 when the Canadian Evidence Act and the Criminal Code were amended to allow persons with disabilities to perform jury duty (Boyle 2011: 19–20). Under Section 627 of the Criminal Code, the judge in a jury trial 'may permit a juror with a physical disability who is otherwise qualified to serve as a juror to have technical, personal, interpretative or other support services' (Criminal Code 1985, § 627).

In Britain, the thirteenth person rule had been a barrier to the use of an interpreter to assist deaf jurors in the jury room until the British Sign Language Act 2022 was passed and came into force on 28 June 2022. The Act recognises British Sign Language (BSL) as a language in England, Wales and Scotland, thereby allowing deaf persons to serve as jurors along with hearing people and a BSL interpreter to enter the jury deliberation room as a thirteenth person (BSL Act 2022). July 2022 saw the first deaf juror at Croydon Crown Court, assisted by BSL interpreters in the deliberation room (Ministry of Justice 2022). As a matter of fact, earlier in August 2019, Britain allowed the first deaf person, Malcolm Johnson, to sit on three juries. Mr Johnson was allowed to perform his jury duty before the passing of the

BSL Act 2022 because he could lip-read and did not need a BSL interpreter in the jury room; he was also able to follow the evidence during the trial in the courtroom by reading the subtitling provided by a court stenographer (Farrell 2019). With the passing of the BSL Act 2022, the issue of an interpreter in the jury room as a thirteenth person has been resolved.

The Australian Capital Territory Government was the first state government in Australia to change its legislation to allow deaf people to serve as jurors in 2018 (Napier et al. 2018). This change is believed to be a result of research conducted over a decade to establish that deaf jurors are capable of performing jury service (Napier et al. 2018). Likewise, the passing of the BSL Act 2022 is believed to be a consequence of the research in this area (British Deaf News 2018; Napier et al. 2018). The decade-long research started with a pilot study to explore the use of sign language interpreting to allow deaf people to serve as jurors. The results of this pilot study demonstrated that deaf mock jurors, with the help of sign language interpreters, performed as well as the hearing jurors in their comprehension of jury instructions (Napier & McEwin 2015; Napier & Spencer 2007, 2008; Napier et al. 2007). It was found that both deaf and hearing jurors equally misunderstood some of the contents, including legal terms and concepts, with insignificant differences in their performance (Napier & McEwin 2015). These findings were confirmed and reinforced by later studies, which showed that deaf jurors were not disadvantaged by accessing the court proceedings via a sign language interpreter (Napier & Spencer 2017). These studies also demonstrated that the participation of deaf jurors did not appear to have any negative impact on the entire trial proceedings, including deliberations (Hale et al. 2017; Napier et al. 2018). The results have led the researchers to conclude that deaf people should be given the same right as hearing persons to perform this civic duty, and that excluding them from jury duty should be considered unlawful discrimination (Hale et al. 2017). As mentioned above, the change in the legislation in the United Kingdom and in the Australian Capital Territory to allow interpreters to assist deaf jurors in court is attributed to the results of these studies.

Interpreting for NES/LEP jurors: Lessons from New Mexico

While sign language interpreters are permitted to assist deaf citizens in participating in jury service in most of the Anglo-American jurisdictions examined above, allowing NES/LEP individuals to serve as jurors with the assistance of interpreters is more the exception than the rule. In the United States, allowing deaf jurors to serve on juries while denying NES/LEP persons the same right has been criticised as inconsistent with the promotion of equality and justice (Chávez 2008; Chávez 2012; Duffy 2017; Gonzales Rose 2011, 2014, 2020; Johnson 2016). Johnson (2016: 973) suggests that providing an interpreter for the deaf but not one for NES/LEP individuals is ‘a distinction without a difference’. Likewise, Kisor (2001) calls for equal treatment of deaf and NES/LEP people, arguing that there is no difference between providing an interpreter for a deaf juror or a foreign language speaker on a functional level.

Excluding NES/LEP individuals from the jury pool is also considered to be a violation of the Sixth Amendment of the US Constitution as well as the principle of trial by one's peers (Brown 1994; Chávez 2008; Chávez 2012; Chernoff 2016; Duffy 2017; Gonzales Rose 2011, 2014, 2020; Johnson 2016). Under the Sixth Amendment of the US Constitution, the defendant has the right to a trial by an impartial jury drawn from a fair cross-section of the community (US Const. amend. VI). It is therefore argued that consistency should be applied to permit NES/LEP persons to perform their civic duty like the deaf, assisted by interpreters (Brown 1994; Chernoff 2016; Gonzales 2014; Johnson 2016).

In the United States, this plea for consistency is strengthened by the fact that in the state of New Mexico, citizens do not have to speak or understand English to be jurors and are entitled to the free assistance of an interpreter (Chávez 2008; Chávez 2012; Duffy 2017; Gonzales Rose 2011, 2014, 2020; Johnson 2016). The state of New Mexico allows NES/LEP persons to serve on grand and petit juries under Article VII, Section 3 of the New Mexico Constitution adopted on 21 January 1911 (Chávez 2008), which has the following provision (NM Const. art VII § 3):

> The right of any citizen of the state to vote, hold office or sit upon juries, shall never be restricted, abridged or impaired on account of religion, race, language or color, or inability to speak, read or write the English or Spanish languages except as may be otherwise provided in this constitution.

In New Mexico, judges do not have the discretion to excuse jurors because of their inability to speak or understand English but have to arrange interpreters to assist jurors' understanding (Chávez 2008). Only when an interpreter speaking a prospective juror's language cannot be obtained after reasonable effort can the juror be excused (ibid.).

In order to ensure quality in the interpretation, courts in New Mexico adopt a series of conducive measures (Chávez 2008). Such measures include the use of certified court interpreters and arranging interpreters to work in pairs and to rotate every 30 to 45 minutes (as in conference interpreting) to prevent interpreter fatigue; interpreters are also allowed to familiarise themselves with the facts of the case beforehand, as well as using wireless audio equipment with headphones (Chávez 2008; Chávez 2012). The use of wireless equipment allows the interpreter to provide interpretation without having to sit close to the juror and to provide the service to multiple users of interpreting services at the same time.

Meanwhile, Chávez's (2012) study found that the participation of NES/LEP jurors and their interpreters did not influence the final verdicts nor compromise the integrity of jury deliberations. Gonzales Rose (2014) suggests that allowing NES/LEP citizens to participate in jury service with the help of an interpreter is appropriate given that over one third of the population of New Mexico speaks a language other than English at home. The census statistics for the year 2022 show that about one quarter of the New Mexican population has limited English proficiency (Migration Policy Institute 2022). It is therefore argued that New Mexico could serve as a useful model for other states in the United States to follow so as to promote equal participation for all (Chávez 2008; Chávez 2012; Duffy 2017; Gonzales Rose 2011, 2014, 2020; Johnson 2016; Kisor 2001). Chávez (2008) argues that since juries in the United States are made up of a mix of citizens of varied educational levels and different personalities and abilities to speak in groups, there is no reason why NES/LEP persons should be automatically excluded from fulfilling their civic responsibility as jurors. Likewise, McCann (2017) suggests that federal and state courts should not disqualify persons with a linguistic limitation but should include them in all judicial proceedings.

Concerns over interpreting for jurors

In reality, the inclusion of NES or LEP jurors in New Mexico remains an exception. In the rest of the US states and other common law jurisdictions where the jury system is in place, a sufficient knowledge of the language of the court remains a fundamental requirement for juror eligibility. Gonzales Rose (2014: 859) identifies four primary concerns about the provision of interpretation for jurors in the United States: jurors not relying on the official English record, risk of inaccuracy in interpretation, a thirteenth person in the jury room and the cost involved. With regard to the first two concerns, Gonzales Rose (2014) points out that court proceedings in the United States often involve testimony given in Spanish or other foreign languages and thus interpretation into English from those foreign languages is nothing out of the ordinary. If the English interpretation is sufficiently reliable to form the basis for criminal convictions and imprisonment, then the interpretation from English to Spanish or other foreign languages should not be an 'insurmountable obstacle' (Gonzales Rose 2014: 861). The concerns in this regard seem to imply a double standard for the quality of interpreting for defendants and for jurors. Regarding the concern about a thirteenth person in the deliberation room, New Mexico has successfully managed NES jurors serving in trials and interpreters in the deliberation room (Gonzales Rose 2014: 863). As a matter of fact, in jurisdictions including the United States, where deaf persons are allowed to serve as jurors assisted by sign language interpreters, concerns about a thirteenth person in the deliberation room have already been allayed. Kisor (2001) identifies the risk of misinterpretation and financial costs as two major objections expressed by opponents to the provision of interpretation services for jurors. He argues that high financial costs should not be used as a reason for discrimination and for excluding NES/LEP people from the jury box. Chávez, a Chief Justice of the Supreme Court of New Mexico, contends that the issues arising from allowing NES citizens to participate in jury service are not unconquerable and the costs involved are not prohibitive. He describes New Mexico's experience with NES jurors as 'pleasantly effective' and argues that NES citizens should not only enjoy the privileges of citizenship but also share in its responsibilities. He suggests that like voting, jury service is a vital civic responsibility that citizens should embrace to demonstrate their patriotism (Chávez 2008: 316).

The rest of this chapter focuses on Hong Kong, the only former British colony in Asia where the jury system is practised to date. It explores the feasibility of providing interpreting services for jurors and discusses the benefits and challenges involved. Specifically, it examines judicial opinions concerning an appeal which contested the trial judge's permission for jurors to access interpretation provided in court and discusses their implications and ramifications.

The practical need for interpreting for jurors in Hong Kong

Advocating for interpretation services for deaf or NES/LEP jurors in the United States and elsewhere is in general driven by the goal of eliminating discrimination and promoting equality. With a focus on the special linguistic landscape in Hong Kong and its implementation of the jury system, this book has provided evidence that interpreting for jurors in Hong Kong not only enhances equal participation but also fulfils a practical need to improve jurors' comprehension, thereby ensuring defendants' right to a fair trial. It has established that the use of English in jury trials has historically limited the jury pool to a small, well-educated population. Results of the study revealed in this book have also demonstrated eligible Chinese jurors' comprehension problems with court proceedings held in English, a language most local jurors speak only as an L2. Besides, despite the almost obligatory provision of Cantonese and English interpretation for defendants and witnesses in English-medium trials, jurors only have partial access to the interpretation provided in court due to the use of the *chuchotage* mode of interpreting, as noted in Chapter 4.

As discussed in Chapter 4, the need for language assistance for jurors was first brought to light in the survey study on jurors' experience in Hong Kong courts by Duff et al. (1992), in which some of the respondents emphasised their need for interpreting services to assist in their understanding. However, it was not until the trial of *Chan Hon Wing* in 2015 (*HKSAR* v. *Chan Hon Wing* 2015) that such a need was articulated in court and a special arrangement was made for jurors to access the interpretation provided in *chuchotage*. This case best illustrates a jury comprehension problem experienced by eligible jurors and thus the need for language assistance. However, the appellate opinions underscore the court's concerns over the quality of interpreting in *chuchotage*. The following section provides a summary of this case and the rulings as well as arguments put forth by the courts in support of their respective decisions.

Appellate decisions and opinions on jurors' access to interpretation

In *HKSAR* v. *Chan Hon Wing* (2015), the trial judge granted the jury's request for some jurors to be provided with wireless headphones to access the Cantonese *chuchotage* interpretation of counsel's closing addresses and the judge's summing-up, which were otherwise audible only to the defendant, as explained in Chapter 4. This special arrangement resulted in an appeal being lodged, first with the Court of Appeal (CA) and subsequently with the Court of Final Appeal (CFA). The ground of appeal was that the arrangement was unprecedented and constituted a material irregularity in the conduct of the trial. It was argued that the arrangement potentially deprived the defendant of a fair trial due to the possibility of inaccurate interpretation in *chuchotage* as the simultaneous nature of *chuchotage* interpreting would inevitably compromise the interpretation quality. It was further submitted that the lack of a record of the *chuchotage* interpretation rendered it impossible to ascertain any misinterpretation problems and thus the verdict was unsafe and unsatisfactory. The CA dismissed the argument of possible misinterpretation as speculative, for the reason that the appellant failed to prove a real or substantial risk of misinterpretation, adding that the interpreter was experienced and competent. The court concluded that the arrangement, though unprecedented, was constitutional as English and Chinese have equal status under Section 3 of the Official Languages Ordinance and dismissed the appeal (*HKSAR* v. *Chan Hon Wing* 2020).

The CA's rejection of the appellant's argument regarding possible misinterpretation is consistent with the 'predominant pattern' observed by Berk-Seligson (1990: 200), where appellate judges tend to uphold rulings of lower courts when appeals are based on alleged interpreter errors or inaccuracies. Berk-Seligson (1990) observes that this pattern exists because the interpretation from the language of the court into a foreign language is often not entered into the court record. Likewise, before the installation of a digital recording system in the mid-1990s in Hong Kong, interpretation out of English into Cantonese or any other dialects or foreign languages was never part of the court record, making it difficult to substantiate any claim about misinterpretation. However, with court proceedings being audio recorded at all court levels in Hong Kong, interpretation into and out of English provided in the consecutive mode is recorded and can be transcribed to become a written court record. Interpretation provided in *chuchotage*, however, remains an exception, as that cannot be captured by the recording system, as noted earlier, which is the subject of the appeal in this case. Following the dismissal of the initial appeal, a further appeal was filed with the CFA and was unanimously allowed, with the convictions quashed and a trial *de novo* ordered.[2] This can be argued to represent a departure from the appellate courts' predominant pattern of upholding lower court rulings on appeals related to interpreter errors or inaccuracies, as observed by Berk-Seligson (1990).

The CFA's ruling focused on the limitations of the *chuchotage* mode of interpreting used in this case (*HKSAR* v. *Chan Hon Wing* 2021). The court accepted the appellant's argument that the absence of a record of the *chuchotage* interpretation rendered it impossible to ascertain what the jurors following the interpretation had actually heard, which raised a concern about whether the arrangement was consistent with the principle of open justice. The CFA suggested that consecutive interpreting (CI) should have been used instead, as it would allow any mistakes to be spotted and an audio record of the interpretation to be kept for later verification. The CFA, however, added that the judgment should not be taken to advocate a total replacement of *chuchotage* with CI, but should be used discretionarily depending on the length of the speech. The CFA's concerns about the possibility of misinterpretation and the lack of a record associated with *chuchotage* are not without merit given the limitations associated with the adoption of this mode of interpreting (Ng 2023). However, the court's ruling and reasoning raise interesting legal and linguistic questions that will be discussed further in the next section.

Implications and possible ramifications of the CFA's ruling and reasoning

Chuchotage has long been one of the common modes of interpreting used in court, with the interpretation typically not being entered into the court record. As explained in Chapter 4, in Hong Kong, *chuchotage* is typically used for interpreting for the defendant during the judge's jury instructions and summing-up, counsel addresses, as well as testimony given in English (without interpreter mediation). This lack of a record was the basis for the CA's dismissal of the initial appeal, as the claim of potential faulty interpretation was deemed speculative without any record to substantiate it. Ironically, the CFA's subsequent ruling in favour of the appellant was also based on the absence of a record of the *chuchotage* interpretation. The CFA held that this lack of a record gave rise to concerns about the principle of open justice and potentially compromised the defendant's right to a fair trial. The CFA's concern raises questions about the suitability of *chuchotage* for the defendant, whose meaningful participation in the trial hinges on effective interpretation. It stands to reason that accuracy and the principle of open justice matter for the defendant as a key stakeholder in the trial just as much as for the jurors who determine the outcome of the trial.

As a matter of fact, there have been other appeals of this kind contesting the accuracy or adequacy of *chuchotage* interpretation provided for defendants. In the case of *HKSAR* v. *Moala Alipate* (2019), the court allowed an appeal advanced on inadequate interpretation provided in the *chuchotage* mode and concluded that the defendant as a result had been deprived of a fair trial. In the case of *HKSAR* v. *Gutierrez Alvarez* (2020), however, a similar claim was advanced but was dismissed by the court, which opined that the appellant failed to prove that the interpretation was inadequate in the first place and how the alleged inadequacy had compromised her right to a fair trial. In both cases, there was no record of the interpretation provided to support or reject the claim. In *Gutierrez*, the court also ruled that the appellant had no right to demand a record of the interpretation, as most courts do not maintain a record of interpretation provided in *chuchotage*, including courts in the United States, the United Kingdom and Singapore. It can be inferred that the absence of a record inherent in the adoption of *chuchotage* can be used by the appellate court to either dismiss an interpreter-related appeal as speculative or otherwise to allow it based on the principle of open justice. This inconsistency in rulings on similar grounds may pose challenges for the application of the principle of *stare decisis*, which binds courts to follow legal precedents. (See Ng 2023 for a detailed discussion of these two cases.)

The remark made by the CFA in *HKSAR* v. *Chan Hon Wing* (2021) on the preferable mode of interpreting in court is likewise problematic as it sends an ambiguous message to the court about the future use of *chuchotage* in court. A further suggestion made by the CFA in this regard is that whether CI or *chuchotage* should be used would depend, in part, on the length of the speech. This view is equally concerning: If the implementation of the open justice principle is crucial to safeguard the defendant's right to a fair trial, why should the length of the speech matter at all? If *chuchotage* is to continue as a mode of interpreting for defendants, it seems to imply a concerning double standard being applied by the courts regarding interpreting for defendants versus interpreting for jurors.

Similarly, the CFA's concerns regarding the potential for misinterpretation in *chuchotage* leading to jurors receiving varying interpretations of the same speech can give rise to significant issues. It is worth noting that the possibility of jurors relying on different versions of the same testimony can also arise even when CI is used. As discussed earlier in this book, in CI settings, jurors are able to hear both the original utterance and its interpretation.

In the United States, bilingual jurors are instructed to ignore testimony given in a foreign language and to consider only the English interpretation (Office of the Executive Secretary 2023). As noted in Chapter 2, following the Supreme Court's decision in *Hernandez* v. *New York* (1991), jurors bilingual in Spanish and English may even be removed from juries in cases involving Spanish and English evidence (see also Rich 2021). Since most jurors in Hong Kong are nowadays bilingual in English and Cantonese to varying degrees, bilingual jurors in Hong Kong are neither removed nor instructed to ignore Cantonese testimony in English-medium trials. Therefore, in witness examination, it is likely that some jurors are listening to the original testimony given in Cantonese, while others are following the English interpretation, especially in the case of a mixed jury comprising both local and expatriate members. In a mixed jury, non-Cantonese-speaking jurors would have to rely on the English interpretation for their comprehension of the testimony given in Cantonese. Similarly, some local jurors experiencing difficulties in understanding counsel's questions asked in English may have to rely on the Cantonese interpretation while others listen to the original English questions. Hence, even in the consecutive mode of interpreting, there is no way to prevent jurors from receiving different versions of the evidence. Therefore, the fact that jurors might be following different versions of the same speech does not seem to be a valid argument for the CFA to allow the appeal.

As noted earlier, court interpreters have long been instrumental in the administration of justice in trials involving litigants who do not speak the language of the court. Unless the contrary is proved, speculating on the possibility of misinterpretation has grave implications for all past and future interpreter-mediated trials and casts unjustified aspersions on the skill of the interpreter. As the Appeal Court in *People* v. *Guzman* (1984; cited also in Brown 1994: 500) notes:

> When any non-English speaking witness (including a defendant) testifies, the entire jury, the judge, the attorneys, the court reporter and, consequently, all future appellate courts, are dependent on the English record

> made by that interpreter. If we do not trust the skills of that person then we have no trial at all.

Indeed, if the skills of the court interpreter cannot be trusted, there should never be interpreter-mediated trials. In Hong Kong, for well over a century and a half, expatriate judges and counsel, in bench trials and in jury trials alike, have long had to rely on the mediation of the interpreter to access testimony given in Cantonese. That misinterpretation might be possible does not mean jurors have to access only unmediated evidence or legal instructions for justice to be done. As Leung (2019: 236) observes, '[i]f unmediated access to evidence is where the bar is set, then many defendants (such as immigrants and other aliens) can never be said to have a fair trial'. The risk of L2 jurors misunderstanding evidence is presumably higher than that of mistranslation by professional interpreters (Leung 2019: 239), which is supported by the findings of my study. Likewise, a study of 48 trials conducted by the New Zealand Law Commission revealed that eight jurors in seven trials with English as their L2 failed to fully understand the evidence. Furthermore, in some cases, this comprehension issue significantly diminished their ability to follow the evidence and participate effectively in deliberations (New Zealand Law Commission 1999). A later study by Smith (2015) on the experience of jurors in New Zealand with migrant and refugee backgrounds and low levels of English ability revealed that despite the fact that LEP jurors can choose to excuse themselves when summoned for jury service, not all of the respondents chose to do so. One respondent said that he chose to accept the service as he highly valued the opportunity to be included, which gave him a sense of belonging, and he believed his language ability would not be a problem. As Leung (2019) points out, prospective jurors may or may not want to serve for different personal reasons, and therefore there may be 'lack of good faith' (Leung 2019: 238) in their self-reported competence of the language. As noted in Chapter 4, in Hong Kong, some people may use LEP as a pretext to avoid jury service, whereas others may not want to admit their lack of language competence either because they are concerned about face or because they consider jury service prestigious. Providing interpreting for jurors could prevent these issues.

Summary and discussion

Trial by jury, whereby members of the community take part in the judicial process as triers of fact, is a cornerstone of the common law system. However, the juror language requirement creates a significant barrier to its implementation by excluding people not equipped with the required language proficiency from the jury pool. In Hong Kong in particular, the juror language requirement restricts jury service to well-educated individuals and compromises the fundamental concept of trial by jury, rendering the jury institution nothing short of symbolic. More importantly and concerningly, presumed language proficiency based primarily on education levels offers no guarantee that Chinese jurors will fully comprehend court proceedings conducted in English. This is effectively illustrated by the case of *Chan Hon Wing*, other anecdotal evidence discussed in Chapter 4, and the findings of the empirical study delineated in this book. These factors underscore the urgent need for extending interpreting services to jurors. While the CA's dismissal of the appeal in *HKSAR* v. *Chan Hon Wing* (2020) could have set a legal precedent for interpreting for jurors, the CFA overruled this potential precedent. The CFA's ruling and reasoning in *HKSAR* v. *Chan Hon Wing* (2021) not only discourage the full extension of this service to jurors but raise questions about the existing practice of court interpreting – a longstanding service in the courts of Hong Kong. Specifically, the CFA's concerns about possible misinterpretation during *chuchotage* and about the lack of a record for verification challenge what has long been legitimately practised – the provision of *chuchotage* for defendants. These concerns suggest a tacit acknowledgement that the adoption of *chuchotage* is not desirable but was tolerable until jurors sought to access it.

This book has shown that extending interpreting services to jurors in need of such assistance is important. Without such support, jurors may struggle to understand proceedings conducted in an L2 in a legal register that even L1 English speakers find difficult to comprehend, as demonstrated in Chapter 3. By extending interpretation services to jurors, the jury pool can be expanded to include individuals with lower education levels, thereby increasing jury representativeness and promoting equal participation. Moreover, unlike in the United States, where the cost associated with providing interpretation for jurors is a major concern (Chávez 2008; Duffy 2017; Gonzales Rose 2014; Kisor 2001), extending the existing interpretation service in Hong Kong would have minimal financial implications. This is because interpreting between English and Chinese in English-medium trials is a standard day-to-day service. Allowing jurors full access to the interpretation provided in court can be easily implemented with the use of appropriate equipment, as demonstrated in the case of *HKSAR* v. *Chan Hon Wing* (2015).

In a nutshell, the need for interpreting for jurors in Hong Kong is evident and long overdue. Continuing to ignore this need at the expense of justice could compromise defendants' right to a fair trial and the principle of trial by jury. This book argues that allowing jurors full access to the interpretation currently provided in court is in the best interests of justice. This would not only help to uphold the principle of trial by jury but would also better safeguard defendants' right to a fair trial. As demonstrated earlier in this chapter, studies examining interpreting for jurors revealed that competent and professionally trained interpreters were able to effectively facilitate the communication of deaf and NES/LEP jurors in court proceedings.

The question is not about whether or not jurors should access interpreter-mediated courtroom discourse, but rather how to ensure that the interpretation provided is accurate and complete for the comprehension of all the parties in court in need of the service. What is important is that the court should make every effort to ensure the highest possible quality of interpreting services in order to avoid compromising the delivery of justice and the defendant's fundamental right to a fair trial.

This will be further discussed in the concluding chapter, which will summarise and evaluate this book, and make recommendations to ensure quality in interpretation and defendants' right to a fair trial.

Notes

1. The examination of this appeal case arises from another research project funded by the Research Grants Council (RGC) of Hong Kong under the General Research Fund (GRF) 2022/23 (Project No. 17600822).
2. At the retrial, the defendant pleaded guilty and was sentenced to a total of 18 years' imprisonment (*HKSAR v. Chan Hon Wing* 2022).

8

Conclusion

Summary of the book

This book commenced with a discussion of the linguistic disadvantage and discrimination facing individuals who do not speak the dominant language in society, with a focus on their participation in jury service. It has been emphasised throughout this book that trial by jury is a key component of a democratic society which works to counteract dictatorship and power abuse by the government. Trial by jury is seen as a fundamental right for a defendant facing serious criminal charges to be tried by his or her peers who are drawn from a cross-section of the community. The participation of ordinary citizens in the judicial process also helps enhance public trust and confidence in the fairness and legitimacy of the legal system. Moreover, engaging ordinary citizens in the judicial process helps foster civic duty and responsibility.

However, the implementation of the jury system is not without challenges. There are concerns over jurors' ability to comprehend convoluted legal discourse presented in court and many Anglo-American countries where the jury system is practised are multi-ethnic and linguistically diverse. In this context, requiring jurors to speak English creates a form of discrimination against those who do not possess the necessary proficiency in the language. This has also been argued to be inconsistent with the principle of trial by jury. These problems are further exacerbated in post-colonial societies where English continues to be used as the dominant language in jury trials, even though it is not the primary language spoken by the local population. This book has provided an overview of the problems related to the implementation of the jury system and the jury comprehension issue, with a particular focus on the post-colonial context of Hong Kong.

This book has revealed that participation in jury trials is exclusive to well-educated people in Hong Kong, and that concerns have been raised about Chinese jurors' ability to understand court proceedings conducted in English, despite their fulfilment of the education-level requirement. It has detailed the first-ever study to use authentic audio recording to test Chinese potential jurors' understanding of court proceedings. The findings of the study demonstrated that those having met the education-level requirement and deemed eligible for jury service struggled to understand court proceedings conducted in English. The comprehension problems were not limited to legal terminology used in court, as non-legal and non-technical language were found to be equally challenging for potential jurors to comprehend. The study also demonstrated that comprehension problems were caused not only by the language used but also by the manner in which the message was articulated, and that L2 English speakers might be particularly susceptible to the latter. It was also found that participants performed far better in reading comprehension than in listening comprehension, presumably due to a lack of exposure to English-speaking environments.

To explore the feasibility of providing interpreting services for jurors, this book has reviewed relevant literature, focusing on sign language interpreting for deaf jurors and the successful experience of New Mexico in providing interpreting services for NES/LEP jurors. It concludes that interpreting for NES/LEP jurors is crucial in the context of Hong Kong. This serves the dual purpose of improving eligible jurors' comprehension and resolving the lack of representativeness in Hong Kong juries. Given that interpreting services between Cantonese and English are routinely provided in English-medium trials for Cantonese-speaking defendants and witnesses, extending existing services to jurors in full is highly feasible; it is merely a technical matter and has minimal financial implications.

In addition to the study exploring potential jurors' ability to understand courtroom discourse, this book has also reviewed appellate opinions on an appeal contesting jurors' access to interpreted legal discourse. While the trial of *HKSAR* v. *Chan Hon Wing* (2015) provides concrete anecdotal evidence corroborating findings from the study, the CFA's ruling (*HKSAR* v. *Chan Hon Wing* 2021) overturned what otherwise would have been a significant legal precedent for interpreting for jurors in Hong Kong. The CFA's ruling and reasoning are primarily based on concerns about the quality of interpretation in *chuchotage*.

Given the findings of the study and the concerns expressed by the CFA, the next section proposes recommendations to address these issues and concerns.

Recommendations

Improving voice projection

The findings of the study documented in this book corroborate earlier research into the use of legalese contributing to jurors' comprehension problems, highlighting the need to use plain language to facilitate jurors' comprehension. Early studies (e.g. Charrow & Charrow 1979; Steele & Thornburg 1991) demonstrated that revised pattern jury instructions using plain English improved jurors' comprehension. This study, employing the use of authentic audio recordings of court proceedings to test potential jurors' understanding, reveals that in addition to discursive voicing, speakers' physical voicing including delivery rate, loudness and clarity of speech also has a significant impact on potential jurors' comprehension of the courtroom discourse. In view of these findings, aside from using language more comprehensible to jurors, judges and counsel should pay particular attention to their physical voicing by speaking slowly, clearly and loudly enough for jurors to comprehend. This is particularly important in the case of Hong Kong because, as noted earlier, most jurors are L2 speakers of the English language. It is equally important that speakers deliver their message in an animated way with the proper use of pauses and intonation rather than in a flat tone. Pauses in speech allow listeners time to digest the speaker's words and make sense of them, while the use of proper intonation makes the speech more engaging and signals key phrases and important information to listeners.

Providing speech scripts for jurors

In view of the finding that Hong Kong jurors' reading comprehension outperformed their listening comprehension of courtroom discourse, I would recommend that speakers where possible provide jurors with speech scripts to assist jurors in their comprehension. Monologues in the courtroom, such as counsels' opening and closing addresses and judges' jury instructions and trial summing-up, are rarely extemporaneous but are often read from some sort of script. Providing jurors with a speech script should not be a difficult technical issue. While there may be some logistical considerations, helping jurors understand the proceedings should be a priority, as jurors are tasked with making important decisions about defendants' guilt or innocence.

Language assistance for jurors

This book highlights a tension between the need to ensure that jurors possess a sufficient command of the English language to understand court proceedings and the upholding of the principle of trial by jury. In light of the findings, the day-to-day interpretation services provided in English-medium trials in Hong Kong should be made fully accessible to any jurors in need of the service. As noted earlier in this book, jurors in the Hong Kong courtroom have long been able to benefit from consecutive interpretation in open court, intended primarily for defendants and witnesses. Therefore, interpreting for jurors is by no means a foreign notion. Allowing jurors to also access interpretation provided in *chuchotage* has the benefit of making court proceedings entirely bilingual for jurors. An entirely bilingual trial makes it possible for more local people without a sufficient command of English to serve on juries, thus promoting equal participation in jury service, in line with the principle of trial by jury.

However, while the results of this study point to Chinese jurors' genuine need for language assistance, which is reinforced by the *HKSAR* v. *Chan Hon Wing* (2015) case discussed in Chapter 7, the CFA's ruling and reasoning in *HKSAR* v. *Chan Hon*

Wing (2021) illustrate the court's major concerns about the quality of interpretation provided in *chuchotage*. It should be noted, however, that the CFA's concerns are not entirely groundless, considering the inherent limitations of *chuchotage*. These limitations include its simultaneous nature, potential acoustic issues and the absence of a recorded interpretation. Nevertheless, *chuchotage* has long been used as the default mode of interpreting out of the court's language and into the language of the defendant, not only in Hong Kong but in most other domestic courts. If there is a concern about the accuracy of interpretation provided in *chuchotage*, how then can it be used as a mode of interpretation for defendants without compromising their right to a fair trial? Instead of denying jurors' access to the interpretation, the court should ensure quality in *chuchotage* interpretation in court proceedings. It is therefore important to explore how this mode of interpreting can be improved to ensure quality in interpreting and the implementation of the open justice principle. This will be further discussed in the following section.

Ensuring quality in interpreting and defendants' right to a fair trial

It is certainly an illusion to assume that the provision of interpreting services is a sufficiently corrective measure to ensure defendants' right to a fair trial (Dingfelder Stone 2018). The quality of the interpretation is what matters. Incompetent interpreting potentially denies the defendant a fair trial (Roberts-Smith 2009). However, as suggested by Ozolins and Hale (2009), quality in interpreting should not be considered the sole responsibility of interpreters. All parties involved in interpreter-mediated communication should assume their share of responsibility to facilitate the work of the interpreter. In the interest of justice and to uphold the principle of trial by jury, it is equally important for both jurors and defendants who require language assistance to be provided with quality interpreting services. The quality of interpretation matters just as much for jurors as it does for defendants. The subsections below discuss the responsibilities of individual parties for ensuring interpretation quality in the context of court interpreting.

Responsibility of the court

Good institutional practice plays a vital role in ensuring quality in interpreting. First of all, it is vital that courts engage only highly capable and professionally trained interpreters. In New Mexico, for example, only certified interpreters are used to assist NES/LEP jurors in the trial and during jury deliberations, and the provision of interpreting services for NES/LEP jurors has been held up as a successful model (Chávez 2008). Similarly, as noted in Chapter 7, studies demonstrate that deaf jurors assisted by professional interpreters are able to understand court proceedings and participate in jury deliberations without being disadvantaged. In the case of Hong Kong, those working in jury trials in the High Court are highly experienced interpreters at the grade of Senior Court Interpreter or otherwise acting in this senior grade. In the case of *HKSAR* v. *Chan Hon Wing* (2015) discussed in Chapter 7, the interpreter had 25 years' experience working with the judiciary at the time of the trial, and was thus described by the Court of Appeal (CA) as 'highly competent, experienced and conscientious' (*HKSAR* v. *Chan Hon Wing* 2020). Note that full-time court interpreters in Hong Kong all start from the grade of Court Interpreter II, and are promoted to the grade of Court Interpreter I after some years of service when considered appropriate. It often takes 15 years or more to move from the lowest to the senior grade.[1] Therefore, the competence of court interpreters in jury trials in Hong Kong should not be a concern.

Nonetheless, engaging competent and qualified interpreters is just a basic and primary step to ensure quality in interpreting. Even the best interpreters can fail to perform well if working conditions are unfavourable. It is therefore important that courts go the extra mile by creating conducive working conditions to enable qualified interpreters to perform to the best of their ability. One good institutional practice is for the court to allow interpreters to access trial-related documents beforehand. It is essential for courts to recognise the interpreter as a member of the court personnel, not an intruder or a necessary evil. As rightly noted by González et al. (2012), attorneys do not appear in court without preparing for their cases in court. It would therefore be unreasonable to expect interpreters to come to court unprepared yet to attain accuracy in interpretation (Ng 2018). Like counsel for the parties, interpreters need time and relevant materials to better prepare for their work. As a matter of fact, allowing interpreters to access relevant documents including speech scripts, if any, is a common practice for conference interpreters and interpreters at the International Criminal Court (ICC) (Stern 2012). Wong's (2019) study demonstrated that interpreters who were given case-related materials to prepare for the trial beforehand performed considerably better than those who had not been given such materials.

Finally, given the limitations of *chuchotage*, it would be worthwhile for the court to consider replacing this mode of interpreting with an electronic mode of simultaneous interpreting (SI) system. Under the electronic mode of SI system, interpreters work in pairs in a sound-proof booth and take turns at regular intervals as their counterparts do in conference interpreting and at the ICC (Stern 2012). This has the benefit of improving acoustics and minimising the impact of *chuchotage* interpretation on participants in court. Stern (2012) even suggests that without the adoption of a fully electronic SI system, it would be unrealistic to expect accuracy in *chuchotage*. As explained in Chapter 4, *chuchotage* interpreting is conventionally conducted in the courtroom with the interpreter sitting or standing close to the defendant who does not speak the language of the court. This can result in acoustic problems for both the interpreter and the defendant, as well as other participants in court because of the murmuring sound, which was also noted by participants in my study. Findings of empirical research support the adoption of an ICC-like SI system to minimise the impact of the interpreter on the proceedings (Hale et al. 2017; Hale et al. 2024). More importantly, the adoption of a fully electronic SI system allows for a full record of the interpretation to be kept and the preservation of a comprehensive transcript of the recording. As noted in Chapter 7, the lack of a record of *chuchotage* interpretation is problematic and could be used to dismiss an alleged interpretation problem as speculative. Conversely, the absence of a record could be cited by the court as a justification for allowing the same allegation due to a lack of transparency and thus a violation of the principle of open justice. A record of the interpretation provided is not only consistent with the principle of open justice, allowing justice to be seen to be done, but also has the advantage of preventing misinterpretation from being used as a convenient ground for appeal and the interpreter from being scapegoated.

Responsibility of the speaker

It must be emphasised that SI is a demanding and highly challenging process. Interpreters working in the simultaneous mode, with or without electronic equipment, are paced by the speakers, thus a fast delivery rate can be a major accuracy impeding factor. My study has demonstrated the negative impact of fast and indistinct speech on the comprehension of jurors. This would presumably also impact on the performance of the interpreter. Therefore, it is important that speakers enunciate their words slowly and clearly to facilitate the work of the interpreter. A notable example can be found in the 1945 Nuremberg war crime trials, where SI in four languages was employed for the first time in court proceedings. To ensure interpretation quality, fast speakers would be signalled with a yellow light to slow down, or a red light to stop and repeat their previous statement (Gaiba 1998: 78–79). The commitment to ensuring interpretation quality demonstrated in the Nuremberg trials is commendable and can serve as an exemplary model for domestic courts.

Responsibility of the interpreter

To maintain high-quality interpretation services, interpreters must endeavour to take responsibility for their own professional development and professionalism (Ozolins & Hale 2009). This includes continually enhancing and updating their language skills, knowledge and interpreting techniques through continuing education, and engaging in self-reflection to identify areas for improvement. As Mikkelson (2017: 146–147) suggests, the start of a career as an interpreter marks the beginning of a lifelong commitment to enhancing knowledge and honing skills. Likewise, it is vital that court interpreters adhere to the code of ethics of the profession by observing impartiality, confidentiality and professional boundaries. When uncertainties or ambiguities arise during the course of interpreting, court interpreters have a duty to clarify these with the speaker rather than resorting to guesswork. Where possible and practicable, interpreters should seek the court's permission before clarifying with the speaker. This demonstrates their commitment to accuracy, transparency and respect for the judicial process while facilitating fair and effective communication within the legal system.

Quality in interpreting is crucial to maintaining the integrity of the judicial process and safeguarding defendants' right to a fair trial. To this end, concerted efforts are required from all responsible parties to ensure that interpreters can 'well and truly interpret' to the best of their 'skill, ability and understanding', as their oath suggests.[2]

Significance of the book and implications for the global context

This book has filled an important void in the existing literature on jury comprehension by exploring an under-researched area in jury comprehension – jurors' ability to understand court proceedings in an L2 – focusing on the unique linguistic landscape in Hong Kong. The findings of the study detailed in this book have implications for the global community, particularly for common law jurisdictions with linguistically diverse populations. The methodology of testing L2 jurors' comprehension of courtroom discourse using authentic audio recording of court proceedings is unprecedented in the field. Previous studies on jury comprehension have hitherto focused on jurors' understanding of legal terminology typically found in jury instructions, relying on textual analyses of standard or pattern jury instructions. These studies have attributed jurors' comprehension problems to speakers' discursive voicing, specifically the use of legalese in the courtroom discourse.

By utilising authentic audio recordings of court proceedings, my study has demonstrated how the speakers' physical voicing of the discourse might have likewise contributed to jurors' comprehension problems and impacted on their reception of the message being projected. This highlights the importance of effective voice projection, in terms of both the language used to convey a message and the manner in which the message is articulated, in order for successful communication to be achieved in both monolingual and bilingual courtroom settings.

This book has also contributed to the debate on the provision of interpreting for NES/LEP jurors by arguing for interpreting services to be provided for jurors in the bilingual legal context of Hong Kong. The study described in this book provides empirical evidence about the challenges facing Chinese jurors in Hong Kong in their comprehension of court proceedings conducted in a language of which they do not have a sufficient command. The results highlight a genuine and pressing need for language assistance to be provided for Chinese jurors in English-medium trials. The provision of interpreting services for jurors serves not only a practical need to assist jurors in their comprehension, but also allows many other people who presently do not meet the language requirement to participate in jury service. Therefore, interpreting for jurors serves both as a micro-level means for improving L2 comprehension within proceedings and as a macro-level strategy for widening judicial participation. This is not particular to Hong Kong, but also applicable to multi-ethnic and multilingual societies around the globe where the jury system is practised, including Australia, Canada, New Zealand, the United Kingdom and the United States. Problems related to the implementation of the jury system in these jurisdictions were examined earlier in this book.

Likewise, concerns about accuracy in interpreting in *chuchotage* apply to all linguistically diverse jurisdictions, where court interpreters have long played a vital role in court. Given that *chuchotage* has been a standard mode of interpreting for defendants in most domestic courts, the need to improve or reform this mode of interpreting is a global concern that is, however, often neglected by the court. It is hoped that this book helps raise awareness of not only the need for interpreting for jurors but also the necessity to ensure the quality of interpreting in order safeguard defendants' right to a fair trial.

Implications for further research

Building on the findings and arguments presented in this book, future research may consider comparing L2 jurors' comprehension of original legal discourse with their comprehension of interpretation provided by professional interpreters. Such a comparison would shed light on the effectiveness of interpreting services and help identify specific areas where comprehension may be compromised.

Furthermore, researchers could further explore the impact of physical voicing on L2 jurors' comprehension of legal discourse. This could involve analysing how comprehension levels vary when the same legal content is delivered by different speakers, focusing on factors such as speech speed, intonation and other prosodic features. By examining these variables, future studies could provide valuable insights into how auditory elements of speech influence understanding among jurors who may already be navigating the complexities of a second language.

Further research in jury comprehension will contribute to improving the implementation of trial by jury and ensuring its continuation as a key institution of the common law system. The ultimate aim is to promote the fairness and efficacy of legal proceedings in increasingly diverse societies and to better safeguard defendants' right to a fair trial.

Notes

1. This is based on my own observations as a former court interpreter and information furnished by retired and serving colleagues, who wish to remain anonymous.
2. Taken from the standard oath for court interpreters in Hong Kong, which reads: 'I, ( ), swear by Almighty God that I am well acquainted with the ( ) language and the English language and that I will well and truly interpret and make explanations to the Court of all such matters and things as shall be required of me to the best of my skill, ability and understanding.'

Appendices

Appendix 1: Study questionnaire

Jury Project
The University of Hong Kong

SECTION A

Questionnaire on Participants' Background and Jury Experience

For each of the following questions, please supply your answer in the space provided or put a tick (✓) in the box which best describes your answer.

Part I. Background information

A1. Age:

- ☐ 21–29
- ☐ 30–39
- ☐ 40–49
- ☐ 50–59
- ☐ 60 or above

A2. Gender:

- ☐ Male
- ☐ Female
- ☐ Other (please specify): ____________________

A3. Occupation (If retired, last occupation):

____

A4. Education (Please select only the highest level attained):
- ☐ Advanced Level (HKALE)
- ☐ Higher Level (HKHLE)
- ☐ Diploma of Secondary Education (HKDSE)
- ☐ IB diploma
- ☐ Associate degree
- ☐ Bachelor's degree
- ☐ Master's degree
- ☐ Doctorate
- ☐ Other/additional qualification: ______________________

A5. Place of birth:
- ☐ Hong Kong
- ☐ Other (Please specify): ____________________

A6. Duration of residence in Hong Kong:

________ years

A7. What is your first language?
- ☐ Cantonese
- ☐ English
- ☐ Other (Please specify): ____________________

A8. Have you ever lived in an English-speaking country for a period of three months or longer?
- ☐ No
- ☐ Yes (Please specify the length): ____________months

A9. How would you rate your **written** English competence?
- ☐ Excellent
- ☐ Good
- ☐ Average
- ☐ Below average
- ☐ Poor

A10. How would you rate your **spoken** English competence?
- ☐ Excellent
- ☐ Good
- ☐ Average
- ☐ Below average
- ☐ Poor

A11. How would you rate your English **listening** competence?
- ☐ Excellent
- ☐ Good
- ☐ Average
- ☐ Below average
- ☐ Poor

A12. How would you rate your English **reading** competence?

- ☐ Excellent
- ☐ Good
- ☐ Average
- ☐ Below average
- ☐ Poor

A13. How often do you **speak** English at HOME?

- ☐ Always
- ☐ Often
- ☐ Sometimes
- ☐ Rarely
- ☐ Never

A14. How often do you **speak** English at WORK?

- ☐ Always
- ☐ Often
- ☐ Sometimes
- ☐ Rarely
- ☐ Never

A15. How often do you **speak** English for communication with FRIENDS?

- ☐ Always
- ☐ Often
- ☐ Sometimes
- ☐ Rarely
- ☐ Never

A16. How often do you **write** in English at WORK?

- ☐ Always
- ☐ Often
- ☐ Sometimes
- ☐ Rarely
- ☐ Never

A17. How often do you **write** in English for communication with FRIENDS?

- ☐ Always
- ☐ Often
- ☐ Sometimes
- ☐ Rarely
- ☐ Never

A18. Have you ever been summoned (i.e. received a notice from the court) to serve as a juror?

- ☐ Yes **(Please continue with Question 19)**
- ☐ No **(End of SECTION A)**

A19. When were you last summoned to serve as a juror?
- ☐ ____________ (Please enter a year)
- ☐ I don't remember

A20. Have you ever served as a juror in a trial?
- ☐ Yes **(Please proceed to Part II)**
- ☐ No **(End of SECTION A)**

End of Part I, SECTION A

Part II. Jury experience

A21. How many times have you served as a juror?
- ☐ Once
- ☐ Twice
- ☐ Three times or more

A22. When did you last serve as a juror?
- ☐ _______ (Please enter a year)
- ☐ I don't remember

A23. How many of these trials in which you served as a juror were conducted in English?
- ☐ _______ (Please enter a number and continue with Question 24)
- ☐ None **(End of SECTION A)**

A24. In the most recent English trial in which you served as a juror:

(i) what was the charge against the defendant?
- ☐ Trafficking in dangerous drugs
- ☐ Murder
- ☐ Rape
- ☐ Other (Please specify): ______________________________
- ☐ I don't remember

(ii) what was the verdict returned by the jury?
- ☐ The defendant was found guilty
- ☐ The defendant was found NOT guilty
- ☐ I don't remember

A25. In the most recent English trial in which you served as a juror, how much did you understand:

(i) the judge's jury instructions at the beginning of the trial?
- ☐ Completely
- ☐ To a great extent
- ☐ Somewhat
- ☐ Very little
- ☐ Not at all

(ii) the lawyers' opening and closing speeches?
- ☐ Completely
- ☐ To a great extent
- ☐ Somewhat
- ☐ Very little
- ☐ Not at all

(iii) the judge's summing-up at the end of the trial?
- ☐ Completely
- ☐ To a great extent
- ☐ Somewhat
- ☐ Very little
- ☐ Not at all

A26. In the most recent English trial in which you served as a juror, did any witness testify in English?
- ☐ Yes (Please continue with Question 27)
- ☐ No (Please go to Question 28)

A27. How much did you understand the evidence given in English without the help of the court interpreter?
- ☐ Completely
- ☐ To a great extent
- ☐ Somewhat
- ☐ Very little
- ☐ Not at all

A28. When a witness gave evidence in Cantonese, assisted by an interpreter, how often did you have to rely on the interpreter's Cantonese interpretation for your understanding of the questions asked in English by lawyers/judges?
- ☐ Always
- ☐ Often
- ☐ Sometimes
- ☐ Rarely
- ☐ Never

A29. In the English trial(s) in which you served as a juror, in what language(s) were the deliberations among the jurors conducted?
- ☐ Cantonese
- ☐ English
- ☐ Other (Please specify): ______________________________

A30. During the deliberations, how often did you have to rely on the help of other jurors for your understanding of the English speeches or evidence given in English?

- ☐ Always
- ☐ Often
- ☐ Sometimes
- ☐ Rarely
- ☐ Never

End of Part II, SECTION A

(End of SECTION A)

SECTION B

Case 1: Murder

You are going to hear recordings extracted from a High Court murder case, including the judge's jury instructions (Part I), the lawyer's opening address (Part II), witness examinations (Parts IIIA and IIIB) and the judge's summing-up (Part IV). You will have to answer some questions after the recording of each speech segment has been played to you. The following are the particulars of the offence.

Court of First Instance, High Court

HKSAR v. [redacted]

Statement of offence:

Murder, contrary to common law and punishable under Section 2 of the Offences against the Person Ordinance, Cap 212. Particulars of offence: [redacted], on the 19th day of August 2006, in Hong Kong, murdered [redacted].

For each of the following questions, please supply your answer in the space provided or put a tick (✓) in the box which best describes your answer. All the answers must be written in **English,** unless otherwise specified.

Part I: Jury instructions

You are about to hear the judge in this case giving instructions to the jury. The recording of this part is 2 minutes and 6 seconds in length. Please answer all the questions in this part at the end of the recording. You may take notes as you wish, to assist your memory.

B1. To what extent did you understand the judge's instructions?

☐ Completely
☐ To a great extent
☐ Somewhat
☐ Very little
☐ Not at all

B2. What do you think are factors causing the comprehension problem, if any? You may choose more than one answer.

☐ The speaker's accent
☐ The speaker's voice was not loud enough
☐ The speaker did not articulate clearly
☐ The speaker spoke too fast
☐ Too many legal terms and concepts
☐ Long sentences
☐ Background noise
☐ Others (Please specify):

☐ No comprehension problem

B3. Explain what 'a verdict' is, OR provide its Chinese equivalent.

B4. How many days will the trial last?

☐ Exactly 7 working days
☐ Longer than 7 working days
☐ Shorter than 7 working days
☐ Around 7 working days
☐ Not sure

B5. Who will choose a jury foreman?

- ☐ The judge
- ☐ The jurors themselves
- ☐ The lawyers
- ☐ Not sure

B6. Who will tell the court the verdict at the end of the trial?

B7. Where will the jury foreman sit once chosen?

- ☐ In the front row nearest to the judge
- ☐ In the front row nearest to the lawyers
- ☐ In the rear row nearest to the defendant
- ☐ Not sure

B8. Who will open the case?

- ☐ The prosecution counsel
- ☐ The defence counsel
- ☐ The judge
- ☐ Not sure

B9. Who has the right to cross-examine the witness called by the prosecution?

- ☐ The prosecution counsel
- ☐ The defence counsel
- ☐ The judge
- ☐ Not sure

B10. Who can re-examine the witness called by the prosecution?

- ☐ The defence counsel
- ☐ The prosecution counsel
- ☐ The judge
- ☐ Not sure

B11. Who will first examine the defendant or his witnesses first?

- ☐ The prosecution counsel
- ☐ The defence counsel
- ☐ The judge
- ☐ Not sure

B12. Who has the right to cross-examine the defendant or any witnesses called by the defence?

- ☐ The prosecution counsel
- ☐ The defence counsel
- ☐ The judge
- ☐ Not sure

B13. How should admitted facts or agreed witnesses' statements be treated?

End of Part I, Case 1, SECTION B

Part II: Opening address

You are about to hear the prosecution counsel giving his opening address in this case. The recording of this part is 4 minutes and 40 seconds in length. Please answer all the questions in this part at the end of the recording. You may take notes as you wish, to assist your memory.

B14. To what extent did you understand the lawyer's speech?

- ☐ Completely
- ☐ To a great extent
- ☐ Somewhat
- ☐ Very little
- ☐ Not at all

B15. What do you think are factors causing the comprehension problem, if any? You may choose more than one answer.

- ☐ The speaker's accent
- ☐ The speaker's voice was not loud enough
- ☐ The speaker did not articulate clearly
- ☐ The speaker spoke too fast
- ☐ Too many legal terms and concepts
- ☐ Long sentences
- ☐ Background noise

☐ Others (Please specify):

☐ No comprehension problem

B16. What is the relationship between Madam [redacted] and the victim?
☐ Landlady and tenant
☐ Divorced couple
☐ Friends
☐ Not sure

B17. Explain what an indictment is or provide its Chinese equivalent.

B18. What was the cause of the dispute between Madam [redacted] and the defendant?

B19. Why did the landlady go to the premises on the 16th August last year?

B20. Who accompanied Madam [redacted] to go to the premises?

B21. According to Madam [redacted], what did the defendant get from the kitchen?

B22. On seeing that, what did the victim do?

B23. Did Madam [redacted] see the defendant attack the victim?

- ☐ Yes
- ☐ No
- ☐ Not sure

B24. Which word was used by the speaker to describe the bleeding of the chop wound on the victim's head? And what does that mean?

B25. What were the defendant and the victim doing when the police arrived?
- ☐ They were struggling over the chopper
- ☐ They were fighting with each other
- ☐ They had stopped fighting
- ☐ Not sure

End of Part II, Case 1, SECTION B

Part IIIA: Examination-in-chief of a witness

You are about to hear the examination-in-chief of an expert witness, a medical doctor who provided treatment to the victim in the hospital. The recording is 1 minute and 12 seconds in length. Please answer all the questions in this part at the end of the recording. You may take notes as you wish, to assist your memory.

B26. To what extent did you understand the questions asked by the lawyer?
- ☐ Completely
- ☐ To a great extent
- ☐ Somewhat
- ☐ Very little
- ☐ Not at all

B27. What do you think are factors causing the comprehension problem, if any? You may choose more than one answer.
- ☐ The speaker's accent
- ☐ The speaker's voice was not loud enough
- ☐ The speaker did not articulate clearly
- ☐ The speaker spoke too fast
- ☐ Too many legal/medical terms and concepts
- ☐ Long sentences
- ☐ Background noise
- ☐ Others (Please specify):

- ☐ No comprehension problem

B28. To what extent did you understand the answers provided by the witness?

- ☐ Completely
- ☐ To a great extent
- ☐ Somewhat
- ☐ Very little
- ☐ Not at all

B29. What do you think are factors causing the comprehension problem, if any? You may choose more than one answer.

- ☐ The speaker's accent
- ☐ The speaker's voice was not loud enough
- ☐ The speaker did not articulate clearly
- ☐ The speaker spoke too fast
- ☐ Too many legal/medical terms and concepts
- ☐ Long sentences
- ☐ Background noise
- ☐ Others (Please specify):

- ☐ No comprehension problem

B30. Explain what a laceration wound is, OR provide its Chinese equivalent.

B31. Where was the victim immediately transferred to from the A & E Department?

B32. What did the doctor do to the victim to stop the bleeding of his wound?

End of Part IIIA, Case 1, SECTION B

Part IIIB: Cross-examination

You are about to hear the cross-examination of the same expert witness. The recording is 3 minutes and 12 seconds in length. Please answer all the questions in this part at the end of the recording. You may take notes as you wish, to assist your memory.

B33. To what extent did you understand the questions asked by the lawyer?

- ☐ Completely
- ☐ To a great extent
- ☐ Somewhat
- ☐ Very little
- ☐ Not at all

B34. What do you think are factors causing the comprehension problem, if any? You may choose more than one answer.

- ☐ The speaker's accent
- ☐ The speaker's voice was not loud enough
- ☐ The speaker did not articulate clearly
- ☐ The speaker spoke too fast
- ☐ Too many legal/medical terms and concepts
- ☐ Long sentences
- ☐ Background noise
- ☐ Others (Please specify):

- ☐ No comprehension problem

B35. To what extent did you understand the answers provided by the witness?

- ☐ Completely
- ☐ To a great extent
- ☐ Somewhat
- ☐ Very little
- ☐ Not at all

B36. What do you think are factors causing the comprehension problem, if any? You may choose more than one answer.

- ☐ The speaker's accent
- ☐ The speaker's voice was not loud enough
- ☐ The speaker did not articulate clearly
- ☐ The speaker spoke too fast
- ☐ Too many legal/medical terms and concepts
- ☐ Long sentences
- ☐ Background noise
- ☐ Others (Please specify):

- ☐ No comprehension problem

B37. Explain what suturing is, OR provide its Chinese equivalent.

B38. Explain what subdural haemorrhage is, OR provide its Chinese equivalent.

B39. What is the defence counsel suggesting to the witness?

- ☐ The doctor should have sutured the scalp of the victim's head more tightly to stop the bleeding
- ☐ The suturing may have caused the problem of subdural haemorrhage
- ☐ They should have detected the problem of subdural haemorrhage earlier
- ☐ Not sure

B40. According to the defence counsel, what might have been the outcome if the doctor had operated on the victim much earlier to deal with the subdural haemorrhage problem?

End of Part IIIB, Case 1, SECTION B

Part IV: Summing-up

You are about to hear the judge giving his summing-up of the case to the jury. The recording is 2 minutes and 14 seconds in length. Please answer all the questions in this part at the end of the recording. You may take notes as you wish, to assist your memory

B41. To what extent did you understand the judge's summing-up?

- ☐ Completely
- ☐ To a great extent
- ☐ Somewhat
- ☐ Very little
- ☐ Not at all

B42. What do you think are factors causing the comprehension problem, if any? You may choose more than one answer.

- ☐ The speaker's accent
- ☐ The speaker's voice was not loud enough
- ☐ The speaker did not articulate clearly
- ☐ The speaker spoke too fast
- ☐ Too many legal terms and concepts
- ☐ Long sentences
- ☐ Background noise

☐ Others (Please specify)

☐ No comprehension problem

B43. What would be a verdict preferred by the court?

B44. Which of the following verdicts will NOT be accepted by the court?
☐ A unanimous verdict
☐ A verdict of 1 to 6
☐ A verdict of 2 to 5
☐ A verdict of 3 to 4
☐ Not sure

B45. What should the jury do if they cannot reach a verdict accepted by the court after a long discussion?
☐ They should continue to discuss the verdict until they have a decision
☐ They should tell the court and the judge will give them further directions
☐ They should tell the court and the judge will then make a decision
☐ Not sure

B46. What is the alternative count of offence to murder the defendant may be convicted of?

B47. If the defendant is convicted of this alternative offence, on which two bases can this offence be?

B48. What is the other separate offence the defendant might be convicted of?

B49. When the jury comes back to the court, who will ask the jury foreman questions in relation to the charge?

- ☐ The judge
- ☐ The court clerk
- ☐ The prosecution counsel
- ☐ Not sure

B50. If the jury finds the defendant guilty of any charge, what will be the first question asked of the jury?

End of Part IV, Case 1, SECTION B

SECTION B

Case 2: Rape

You are going to hear recordings extracted from a High Court rape case, including the judge's jury instructions (Part I), the lawyer's opening address (Part II) and the judge's summing-up (Part III). You will have to answer some questions after the recording of each speech segment has been played to you. The following are the particulars of the offence.

Court of First Instance, High Court

HKSAR v. [redacted]

Statement of offence:

Rape, contrary to Section 118(1) of the Crime Ordinance, Cap 200. Particulars of offence, [redacted], on the 30th of August, 2006, at Room [redacted], Choi Wan Estate, Wong Tai Sin, Kowloon, in Hong Kong, raped [redacted].

For each of the following questions, please supply your answer in the space provided or put a tick (✓) in the box which best describes your answer. All answers must be written in **English**, unless otherwise specified.

Part I: Jury instructions

You are about to hear the judge in this case giving instructions to the jury. The recording of this part is 3 minutes and 6 seconds in length. Please answer all the questions in this part at the end of the recording. You may take notes as you wish, to assist your memory.

B51. To what extent did you understand the judge's instructions?

- ☐ Completely
- ☐ To a great extent
- ☐ Somewhat
- ☐ Very little
- ☐ Not at all

B52. What do you think are factors causing the comprehension problem, if any? You may choose more than one answer.

- ☐ The speaker's accent
- ☐ The speaker's voice was not loud enough
- ☐ The speaker did not articulate clearly
- ☐ The speaker spoke too fast
- ☐ Too many legal terms and concepts
- ☐ Long sentences
- ☐ Background noise

☐ Others (Please specify):

☐ No comprehension problem

B53. What is the word used by the judge to describe the system of justice practised in Hong Kong?

B54. Which of the following is a characteristic of this justice system?

☐ The judge plays an active role in the examination of witnesses
☐ The judge plays a passive role in the examination of witnesses
☐ The prosecution and the defence counsel play a passive role in the examination of witnesses
☐ Not sure

B55. According to the judge, what are the two important principles of the Hong Kong system of criminal law and justice?

B56. According to the judge, what does 'being satisfied beyond reasonable doubt' about the defendant's guilt mean?

End of Part I, Case 2, SECTION B

Part II: Opening address

You are about to hear the prosecution counsel giving his opening address in this case. The recording of this part is 4 minutes and 7 seconds in length. Please answer all the questions in this part at the end of the recording. You may take notes as you wish, to assist your memory.

B57. To what extent did you understand the lawyer's speech?

- ☐ Completely
- ☐ To a great extent
- ☐ Somewhat
- ☐ Very little
- ☐ Not at all

B58. What do you think are factors causing the comprehension problem, if any? You may choose more than one answer.

- ☐ The speaker's accent
- ☐ The speaker's voice was not loud enough
- ☐ The speaker did not articulate clearly
- ☐ The speaker spoke too fast
- ☐ Too many legal terms and concepts
- ☐ Long sentences
- ☐ Background noise
- ☐ Others (Please specify):

- ☐ No comprehension problem

B59. What was the relationship between the victim and the defendant?

- ☐ The victim was the defendant's sister
- ☐ The victim was the ex-girlfriend of the defendant's sister
- ☐ The victim was the defendant's ex-girlfriend
- ☐ Not sure

B60. Why did the victim return to the flat where she used to live?

B61. Why was the victim unable to enter the flat initially?

B62. Where did the victim wait for Ms [redacted] to come back?

- ☐ Outside the flat
- ☐ Inside the flat
- ☐ In an area close to the flat
- ☐ Not sure

B63. Why did the victim decide to take a nap?

B64. What did the defendant do to the victim before kissing her?

- ☐ He took off her clothing
- ☐ He made her lie on bed
- ☐ He chatted with her
- ☐ Not sure

B65. What did the victim do when the defendant started to kiss her?

- ☐ She shouted for help
- ☐ She resisted his advances by pushing him away
- ☐ She said no and tried to push him away
- ☐ Not sure

End of Part II, Case 2, SECTION B

Part III: Summing-up

You are about to hear the judge giving his summing-up to the jury. The recording of this part is 2 minutes and 37 seconds in length. Please answer all the questions in this part at the end of the recording. You may take notes as you wish, to assist your memory.

B66. To what extent did you understand the judge's summing-up?

☐ Completely
☐ To a great extent
☐ Somewhat
☐ Very little
☐ Not at all

B67. What do you think are factors causing the comprehension problem, if any? You may choose more than one answer.

☐ The speaker's accent
☐ The speaker's voice was not loud enough
☐ The speaker did not articulate clearly
☐ The speaker spoke too fast
☐ Too many legal terms and concepts
☐ Long sentences
☐ Background noise
☐ Others (Please specify)

☐ No comprehension problem

B68. According to the judge, for the defendant to be found guilty of the offence of rape, what does the prosecution have to prove?

☐ The defendant had unlawful sexual intercourse with the victim
☐ The defendant had sexual intercourse with the victim without her consent
☐ At the time of sexual intercourse, the defendant knew that the victim did not consent to it, or did not care whether she consented to it or not
☐ Not sure

B69. Does the defendant dispute that sexual intercourse occurred?

☐ Yes
☐ No
☐ Not sure

70. Explain the difference between consent and submission, OR provide their Chinese equivalents.

B71. According to the judge, what can be the causes of submission?

B72. Explain the meaning of 'reckless', OR provide its Chinese equivalent.

End of Part III, Case 2, SECTION B

(End of SECTION B)

SECTION C

Excerpt of summing-up

Please read the following text excerpted from the judges' summing-up in the murder case and answer the questions that follow.

Now you have heard that the defendant has two previous convictions. Normally the jury doesn't hear about the previous convictions of the defendant because except in certain special circumstances, they are irrelevant to the offence or offences with which they are charged. And reference to previous convictions might give rise to the risk of the jury assuming unfairly that because he has committed offences in the past, he is not telling the truth or that he must be guilty of the offence charged now.

Here the defendant puts his record before you to show that he is being frank about what he tells you. You know that his previous offences are very old, 1974 and 1989 and they are very minor. They are not offences of violence and are punished by small fines. The fact that the defendant has a record doesn't mean that he can't tell the truth or that he must be guilty of the offence. They are not relevant to the likelihood of his having committed the present offence. He told you about them to show you that after these offences he lives a blameless life. And they are relevant only to the question of credibility, and it's for you to decide about his credibility. You could effectively treat him as a man of clear record for the purposes of this hearing.

C1. To what extent did you understand this excerpt of the judge's summing-up?

- ☐ Completely
- ☐ To a great extent
- ☐ Somewhat
- ☐ Very little
- ☐ Not at all

C2. Explain what 'the previous convictions of a defendant' means, OR provide its Chinese equivalent.

C3. According to the judge, what impact might a defendant's previous convictions have on the jury in assessing the defendant's credibility and likelihood to commit the present offence?

C4. Explain what 'punished by small fines' means, OR provide its Chinese equivalent.

C5. Explain what 'a man of clear record' means, OR provide its Chinese equivalent.

End of SECTION C

(END OF TEST)

Thank you for your participation!

Appendix 2: Audio transcripts

To enhance readability, the transcripts of the monologues provided here omit transcription keys that represent prosodic features of speech.

Case 1: Murder

Part I: Jury instructions

Now, members of the jury, you've been chosen as jurors to consider the facts of this case and eventually to return a verdict as to whether this defendant is guilty or not guilty of the offence of murder with which he has been charged.

Now I told you earlier that it is expected that this trial lasts around seven working days. But I'll remind you that's an estimate. It may be slightly shorter; it may be a bit longer. But it's the best estimate that we can devise at the present time. Shortly I'm going to release you for half an hour so that you can telephone your family and your colleagues to tell them that you've been chosen for jury duty and to make any arrangements that you need to make immediately.

During that time or before court finishes today, I'll ask you to choose from among yourselves one person to act as your foreman. The person that you choose will be the person who— will be your spokesman if you want to say anything to me, or if you need to ask necessary questions, and it will be that person, male or female, who will tell the court your verdict at the end of the trial.

Once you've chosen the foreman, I'll ask that person to sit in the front row nearest to me please.

You're probably unfamiliar with the court proceedings and I'll give you a bit of information about them. The procedure will be that the prosecution counsel will open the case to you by telling you what this case is about. He will call his witnesses and examine his witnesses.

Defence counsel has the right to cross-examine the witness and the prosecution may examine if necessary.

At the end of the prosecution case, the defendant may give evidence or call witnesses. If so, the defendant and any witnesses that might be called will be examined by defence counsel first, then crossed-examined by prosecution counsel, and if necessary re-examined on the—by defence counsel.

During the trial, there may be statements read out to you with the agreement of both sides; there may be admissions of certain facts. Any agreed witness statements or agreed facts will be just as much evidence for you to take into account in reaching your verdict as it would be—as if the witness had been called to give oral evidence about these matters.

Once all the evidence is in front of you, counsel will address you about the respective cases. I'll then sum up and direct you about the law. After that, you'll go out and consider your verdict.

Part II: PC opening speech

The events fundamentally concern three persons, obviously, the accused, [redacted], the victim, [redacted], and the victim's ex-wife, a Madam [redacted], and, if you just turn over the indictment, you'll see a page that has a list of witnesses here.

And Madam [redacted]— [redacted], will be the first prosecution witness. She will be called shortly to give evidence orally to you. She will tell you that in late 2005 through an estate agency she rented an apartment she owned in a building in Tai Nan Street to the defendant. She will tell you that the rent was paid properly for many months. But then in the middle of last year, problems arose in relation to the payment of rent.

Uh, in fact there was a dispute between her as the landlady and the accused, who was the tenant of this flat on the 3rd floor of this building. She will go into some detail and I won't summarise now the dispute, but she will tell you how a dispute arose, that was over the repair of an air-conditioner, or a leaking air-conditioner. And the dispute went on for some weeks, and in the end the accused said he was not going to pay rent until the dispute was settled.

She will tell you how—uh— she tried to get the arrears of the rent paid. But finally on the evening of the 16th of August last year, she was owed some several thousand dollars in arrears and she went around to the apartment to see the accused and talk about the money that was owed.

And she will tell you that she took with her, her ex-husband, the victim. Well, they arrived at the premises, uh, they gained entry and uh conversations occurred between them. An argument developed.

And Madam [redacted] will tell you that she saw the accused go to the kitchen of the premises and pick up a chopper, an item which is common enough in Hong Kong, and you've all seen them before. She will tell you that the accused came out of the kitchen with the chopper, uh on seeing this, she will tell you that, her ex-husband tried to leave the premises, uh, he exited. And she will tell you that he was chased by the accused, armed with the chopper down the stairs leading from the third floor to the ground floor.

Uh, she was a little behind them. She didn't actually see them going down the stairs. By the time she got to the ground floor, she could see her ex-husband and the defendant grappling over the chopper.

And she will tell you that there was clearly, uh, a chop wound on the—uh, her ex-husband's head and he was bleeding profusely.

She had a mobile phone with her. She immediately called the police. The police soon arrived and they called for both the, uh, accused and victim to stop the struggle over the chopper, which they did.

The police organised for an ambulance to take the, uh, victim, Mrs [redacted]'s ex-husband to the hospital. He was taken to the Kwong Wah Hospital. You can see from the back of the indictment, that uh various doctors' names appear there. You will hear from one or more of these doctors that will tell you the medical treatment that was given to the victim Mr. [redacted] over the next few days. Unfortunately his condition deteriorated and on the 19th of August he died.

Part IIIA: Examination-in-chief of PW (medical doctor)

PC: Well, tell us what happened. Well, first of all, tell us (.) how it came about that the patient came up to see you. What happened?

PW: So the patient was er arrived at about er eleven p.m. At that time I was working (.) er in the same ward. So I was er called upon by the nurse to er assess the patient. I attend the patient immediately. And er I know from the (.) er A&— (.) er Emergency doctor (.) e::r (.) er Doctor [redacted], and also from the patient that, the pati— (.) er the patient er (.) d— did er suffer from er (.) er chop wound injury (.) over the left side of the head. And (.) er resulting in a big laceration wound, and er (.) they were resulting in a massive blood loss. It mean a lot of blood was being e:r (.) er lost before admission to the hospital. And e::r in the Emergency Department the blood pressure was low, and er (.) e:::r (.) and he was being resuscitated, and was er transferred immediately to the neurosurgical ward.

PC: Er— (.) how did you go about the resuscitation?

PW: Yeah. So e:r— e::r— (.) we er I so I er immediately arrange er er (.) er continue the (.) the transfusion by er transfusing er (.) crystalloid, and also er transfusion of er (.) blood products. And er I also er tried to er control the bleeding (.) by er suturing the scalp.

Part IIIB: Cross-examination of PW (medical doctor)

DC: Well, if your suturing is very effective, and that would then build up a pressure on the brain. The pressure would be excessive on the brain instead of escaping through the suture.

PW: (2.5) I'm sorry? Can you:: repeat?

DC: If your suturing is highly effective, one hundred per cent effective, but nevertheless below it, some further bleeding or pressure develops, if it can't es—if that pressure can't escape through the suture holes, the pressure would be applied to the brain.

PW: (2) Mmm. (1) An::d (2) actually we e:::r (.) actually I— (.) I er (2) I'm sorry, can you (.) can you=

DC: =Well, in this case we hear that, eventually, when the head was opened up at some time after six a.m., the pressure was such that the brain was displaced slightly to one side.

PW: Yes.

DC: Right? What I'm saying is that er, if there was no drain and the sutures were totally effective, any further development of pressure (.) beneath the sutures would have nowhere to escape.

PW: (6) Actually the su— the:: (.) the scalp was sutured in the full thickness, and the:: the— the— the bleeding was er (.) e::r (.) was stopped by that, so e:: r (.) you mean er (2) and (2.5) and e::r (2) actually I'm— I'm quite— I'm not quite understand your question. Can you er (.) er repeat it again?

DC: Well, did you— (1.5) you now know the sequence of events that led to the death of the accused by reading the hospital notes, [don't you?

PW: [Mm hmm. Yes. Yes. Yes.

DC: Right?

PW: Yes.

DC: And— and— it's right, isn't it, that er (.) by the time the surgeon, as it were, got access to the brain, the patient was er (1.5) more or less brain dead, (5) do you agree?

PW: E::r (.) yes.

DC: Yeah. And so, with the benefit of hindsight, I'm not disputing everybody doing the best they could under these circumstances, but (.) it would have been better, would it not, having regard to what we now know, to have dealt with that subdural haemorrhage, as soon as possible after it was first (known)?

PW: (8) <silence>

DC: Do you agree?

PW: Erm (.) erm I'm sorry, can you=

DC: =Well, the subdural (.) haemorrhage was detected (1) in the first brain scan (.) at about one twenty a.m., right?

PW: Yes.

DC: But, but nothing was done about it (.) until much later, after it had (.) enlarged…

PW: Mmm.

DC: …right?

PW: E::r

DC: All I'm saying is that, had the subdural haemorrhage been dealt with surgically (.) much earlier on, this patient would have stood a much better chance of survival.

Part IV: Summing-up by judge

Now, you will shortly retire to consider your verdict. It's desired that you should all agree on your verdict but if you can't all agree, the court will accept verdicts of 6 to 1 or 5 to 2. But there must be at least five of you who are agreed. You will be asked for the verdict on the individual charge on which all seven of you have—, seven of you have agreed on it. And if you are not all agreed, uh, in agreement, you will be asked whether your decision is 6 to1 or 5 to 2.

A, a verdict of 3:4 either way is not a verdict that I will be able to accept. Unless after a long discussion you couldn't reach a verdict other than 3 to 4, you will tell me about it and I will direct you further. But at this stage, that's not a matter you have to concern yourself with.

When you come back into court, Mr Foreman will be asked a series of questions with respect to the charge, so that your verdict can be delivered in a way that avoids mistakes or misunderstandings. You will be given a typed copy of the questions you will be asked. I suggest that you put your name on your own copies and that you um bring your own copies back to court when the foreman announces your decision to the court.

So you've got one relating to the count of murder, one relating to the alternative count of manslaughter. And you will be asked on what basis you deliver your verdict of manslaughter or whether it is on a basis of unlawful act, or whether it is on the basis of provocation.

And I've also put into a separate one in respect of the possibility of wounding. So please bring your own copies back to court and if any mistakes are made when the foreman reads out your answers, you can bring it to my attention straight away.

I will explain what will happen when you come back to court. Mr Foreman will be asked to stand up and then the clerk will ask the questions for the charges as set out on those forms.

If your verdict is not guilty on the charge, that's the end of your task. If your verdict is guilty of any charge, you'll be asked whether the verdict is one on which you all agree, and if it's not one on which you all agree, by what majority have you reached the verdict.

When you leave here, you will be taken by the jury usher to your deliberating room which is a different one from the one you've been using during the trial.

Case 2: Rape

Part I: Jury instructions

The system of justice which we practise is adversarial in nature, which means that the presentation and examination of witnesses is substantially in control of counsel for prosecution and counsel for the defence. Subject to certain rules, which I enforce, you and I as impartial judges sit and listen to what counsel say and what the witnesses have to say when they are giving their evidence.

Now throughout the trial you must keep in mind two very important principles of the, the Hong Kong system of criminal law and justice. These are fundamental to the trial. The first of these is that the prosecution must prove the accused's guilt. He does not have to prove his innocence.

The second of these is that before you may convict the accused, you must be satisfied beyond reasonable doubt that he is guilty. That is the same thing as being sure of his guilt. Nothing less than that will do.

Although you are perfectly entitled to discuss the case amongst yourselves when you are in your jury room during the course of the trial, what I would emphasise you must not do is come to any premature conclusion. The time for you to come to a conclusion as to whether the accused is guilty is when you retire to consider your verdict at the end of the trial. By that stage you will have heard all the evidence and the arguments of both counsel as well as my directions on the law. You will then be in a much better position to exchange views and arrive at a fair conclusion.

The conclusion you reach must of course be based on the evidence you hear in this court and only on that evidence. That means you mustn't discuss the case with anyone, nor allow anyone outside of your fellow jurors to discuss the case with you. It is especially important, and I appreciate it's especially difficult in respect of your family and your friends. But you must not discuss the case with them when you get home or in the course of your social activities.

Part II: PC opening

Now the alleged victim, a Ms [redacted], had been having a lesbian relationship with the younger sister of the accused. The younger sister's name was [redacted]. As a result, Ms [redacted] had been living at the accused's residence with [redacted] for over a year.

Now, that relationship had turned sour, however, and the two girls terminated their relationship in July of 2006. It was agreed that Ms [redacted] would pick—, would pack up her stuff and leave. On the day in question, Ms [redacted] returned to that residence with the intention to do just that, that is, to collect her stuff and go.

Initially, she could not get in, as she no longer had the keys to the premises. She waited for about two hours in the vicinity of the premises, as she was led to believe that [redacted] was not inside, and she did not wish to disturb her other family members.

However, at about 2pm, she could wait no longer, so Ms [redacted] knocked on the door. The accused open the door. She got in and began her packing. As she was packing, the accused chatted with her. Some time later, she finished packing, then she wrote a goodbye note to [redacted], using stationery found at the premises. After that, she felt a bit sleepy, and decided to take a nap, and at the same time used that opportunity to wait for the return of [redacted]'s mother, so as to greet her. Ms [redacted] then took to the upper bunk of the bunk bed in [redacted]'s room.

After Ms [redacted] had lain down for a while, the accused climbed onto the ladder that was beside the bed, and started chatting with her again. Then at some point, the accused started to kiss Ms [redacted] by force, and against her will. Ms [redacted] attempted to resist his advances by saying no and pushing him away. However, she failed in her attempts to push him away. The accused eventually climbed onto the bed, took off Ms [redacted]'s clothing, and had sexual intercourse with her against her will.

Part III: Judge's summing-up

What then is rape? A man commits rape if he has unlawful sexual intercourse with a woman, who at the time does not consent to it, and if, at the time he has sexually intercourse with her, he either knows that she does not consent to it, or is reckless as to whether she consents to it.

So before you may convict the accused of the charge of rape, you have to be sure of three things.

Firstly, that he had sexual intercourse with Ms [redacted]. Now you don't have to worry at all about the word 'unlawful' in the context of this case. It's an admitted fact in this matter that intercourse occurred, so you will have no difficulty in finding this evidence proved.

Secondly, that at the time of that sexual intercourse, Ms [redacted] did not consent to it. The word consent bears its ordinary meaning. You'll appreciate that there is a difference between consent on the one hand and mere submission on the other. If a woman is not willing to have sexual intercourse, but she submits to it, whether as a result of threats, or as a result of force, or as a result of fear of violence, or as a result of intimidation, or anything of that nature, her submission is not consent.

Thirdly, that at the time of sexual intercourse, the accused knew either that Ms [redacted] did not consent, or he was reckless as to whether she consented. And in this context, the prosecution has to prove that the accused had a guilty mind, in the sense that he knew that Ms [redacted] did not consent, or that he was reckless as to whether she consented.

Appendix 3: Transcription keys used in this book

Key	Meaning
(2)	A pause in seconds
(.)	A brief pause of less than half a second
::	Prolonged sound, indicated by the length of the row of colons
—	Incomplete utterance or false start
[	Start of an interruption and the utterance which is interrupted
boldface	Words in boldface indicate where stresses are placed
...	Indication of an unfinished utterance or continuation of an unfinished utterance from the previous turn
<words>	Words in angle brackets indicate transcriber's description
=	Latched utterances (i.e. no pause between turns)

References

Abramson, J. (1994). *We, the jury: The jury system and the ideal of democracy*. Basic Books.

Agresti, A. (2018). *Statistical methods for the social sciences* (5th ed.). Pearson.

Altenberg, E. P. (2005). The perception of word boundaries in a second language. *Second Language Research*, *21*(4), 325–358. https://doi.org/10.1191/0267658305sr250oa

Andersen, P. A. (2008). *Nonverbal communication: Forms and functions* (2nd ed.). Waveland Press Inc.

Baguley, C., McKimmie, B., & Masser, B. (2020). Re-evaluating how to measure jurors' comprehension and application of jury instructions. *Psychology, Crime & Law*, *26*(1), 53–66.

Bell, A. (1984). Language style as audience design. *Language in Society*, *13*(2), 145–204. https://doi.org/10.1017/S004740450001037X

Bell, A. (2002). Back in style: Reworking audience design. In P. Eckert & J. R. Rickford (Eds.), *Style and sociolinguistic variation* (pp. 139–169). Cambridge University Press. https://doi.org/10.1017/CBO9780511613258.010

Berk-Seligson, S. (1990). *The bilingual courtroom: Court interpreters in the judicial process*. University of Chicago Press.

Berk-Seligson, S. (2009). *Coerced confessions: The discourse of bilingual police interrogations*. Mouton de Gruyter. https://doi.org/10.1515/9783110213492

Boersma, P., & Weenink, D. (2022). Praat: *Doing Phonetics by Computer* [Computer program]. Version 6.3.03. https://praat.org

Boyle, C. (2011). Consideration of the eligibility of blind or deaf people for jury service in Ireland. *Hibernian Law Journal*, *10*, 1–40.

Breay, C., & Harrison, J. (2014, July 28). *Magna Carta: An introduction*. British Library. https://brewminate.com/magna-carta-an-introduction/

British Deaf News. (2018, April 10). *Heriot-Watt professor wins top honour*. https://www.britishdeafnews.co.uk/heriot-watt-professor-wins-top-honour/

Brown, C. L. (1994). A challenge to the English-language requirement of the juror qualification provision of New York's judiciary law. *New York Law School Law Review*, *39*(3), 479–510.

Brown-Blake, C., & Chambers, P. (2007). The Jamaican creole speaker in the UK criminal justice system. *The International Journal of Speech, Language and the Law*, *14*(2), 269–294. https://doi.org/10.1558/ijsll.v14i2.269

Calvert, D. R. (1986). *Descriptive phonetics* (2nd ed.). Thieme.

Cameron, N., Potter, S., & Young, W. (1999). The New Zealand jury. *Law and Contemporary Problems*, *62*(2), 103–139. https://doi.org/10.2307/1192254

Charrow, R. P., & Charrow, V. R. (1979). Making legal language understandable: A psycholinguistic study of jury instructions. *Columbia Law Review*, *79*(7), 1306–1374. https://doi.org/10.2307/1121842

Chávez, E. L. (2008). New Mexico's success with non-English speaking jurors. *Journal of Court Innovation*, *1*, 303–327.

Chávez, H. L. (2012). *Examining the effects of the inclusion of non-English speaking jurors on jury verdicts and juror experiences* [Unpublished doctoral dissertation]. University of Nevada, Reno.

Chernoff, N. W. (2016). No records, no right: Discovery & the fair cross-section guarantee. *Iowa Law Review*, *101*(5), 1719–1785.

Cheung, K. M. (2012). *Trial by jury: The reform of the jury system in Hong Kong* [Doctoral dissertation, City University of Hong Kong]. CityU Theses Online. http://lbms03.cityu.edu.hk/theses/abt/jsd-slw-b42002680a.pdf

Chushi she jian an li qi tian yingwen shenxun peishen tuan tuiting hou shi jie bu ming 'acquit' dian jie 廚師涉姦案歷 7 天英文審訊 陪審團退庭後始揭不明「Acquit」點解 [Chef's rape case: 7-Day English trial reveals jurors' comprehension problem with 'acquit' during deliberations]. (2017, July 19). *Mingpao News*. https://shorturl.at/mowHO

Clark, W. (1923). Magna Carta and trial by jury. *North Carolina Law Review*, *2*(1), 1–13.

Cotterill, J. (2003). *Language and power in court: A linguistic analysis of the O. J. Simpson trial*. Palgrave Macmillan. https://doi.org/10.1057/9780230006010

Davies, C., & Edwards, C. (2004). 'A jury of peers': A comparative analysis. *The Journal of Criminal Law*, *68*(2), 150–159.

Davison, C. B. (2020). The quest for representative juries in the Northwest Territories. *The Northern Review*, *50*. https://doi.org/10.22584/nr50.2020.009

Department of Justice. (2023). *Key figures and statistics*. https://www.doj.gov.hk/en/about/stat.html

Devlin, P. (1956). *Trial by jury*. Stevens.

Dingfelder Stone, J. H. (2018). *Court interpreters and fair trials*. Springer International Publishing. https://doi.org/10.1007/978-3-319-75355-3

Duff, P., Findlay, M., & Howarth, C. (1990). The Hong Kong jury: A microcosm of society? *The International and Comparative Law Quarterly*, *39*(4), 881–891. https://doi.org/10.1093/iclqaj/39.4.881

Duff, P., Findlay, M., Howarth, C., & Chan, T. F. (1992). *Juries: A Hong Kong perspective*. Hong Kong University Press.

Duffy, K. P. (2017). Lost in translation: New Mexico's non- English speaking jurors and the right to translated jury instructions. *New Mexico Law Review*, *47*(2), 376–400.

Dumas, B. K. (2000). US pattern jury instructions: Problems and proposals. *Forensic Linguistics*, *7*(1), 49–71. https://doi.org/10.1558/sll.2000.7.1.49

Evans, J. D. (1996). *Straightforward statistics for the behavioral sciences.* Brooks/Cole Publishing Company.

Farrell, M. (2019, August 30). Breakthrough as deaf juror is called for service in UK. *Law Society Gazette, Ireland.* https://www.lawsociety.ie/gazette/top-stories/2019/08-august/first-deaf-juror-serves-on-three-juries-in-a-row

Frank, J. (1930). *Law and the modern mind.* Brentano's.

Gaiba, F. (1998). *The origins of simultaneous interpretation.* University of Ottawa Press.

Gibbons, J. (2017). Towards clearer jury instructions. *Language and Law / Linguagem e Direito*, *4*(1), 142–160.

Gonzales Rose, J. B. (2011). The exclusion of non-English-speaking jurors: Remedying a century of denial of the Sixth Amendment in the federal courts of Puerto Rico. *Harvard Civil Rights-Civil Liberties Law Review*, *46*, 497–549. https://journals.law.harvard.edu/crcl/wp-content/uploads/sites/80/2009/06/Rose.pdf

Gonzales Rose, J. B. (2014). Language disenfranchisement in juries: A call for constitutional remediation. *Hastings Law Journal*, *65*(3), 811–864.

Gonzales Rose, J. B. (2020). Color-blind but not color-deaf: Accent discrimination in jury selection. *New York University Review of Law and Social Change*, *44*(3), 309–354.

González, R. D., Vásquez, V. F., & Mikkelson, H. (2012). *Fundamentals of court interpretation: Theory, policy, and practice* (2nd ed.). Carolina Academic Press.

Hale, S. B., Martschuk, N., Ozolins, U., & Stern, L. (2017). The effect of interpreting modes on witness credibility assessments. *Interpreting: International Journal of Research and Practice in Interpreting*, *19*(1), 69–96. https://doi.org/10.1075/intp.19.1.04hal

Hale, S., Martschuk, N., Goodman-Delahunty, J., & Lim, J. (2024). Juror perceptions in bilingual interpreted trials. *Perspectives*, 1–24. https://doi.org/10.1080/0907676X.2024.2343772

Heffer, C. (2005). *The language of jury trial: A corpus-aided analysis of legal-lay discourse.* Palgrave Macmillan.

Heffer, C. (2018). When voices fail to carry: Voice projection and the case of the 'dumb' jury. In J. H. C. Leung & A. Durant (Eds.), *Meaning and power in the language of law* (pp. 207–235). Cambridge University Press. https://doi.org/10.1017/9781316285756.010

Hogg, K. (2021). Seeing justice done: Increasing Indigenous representation on Canadian juries. *Appeal*, *26*(51), 53–70.

Hong Kong Government. (1854). Jury list for 1854. *The Hong Kong Government Gazette.* https://sunzi1.lib.hku.hk/hkgro/view/g1854/727405.pdf

Hong Kong Government. (1858). Jury list for 1858. *The Hong Kong Government Gazette*. https://sunzi1.lib.hku.hk/hkgro/view/g1858/724572.pdf
Hong Kong Government. (1879). Jury list for 1879. *The Hong Kong Government Gazette*. https://sunzi1.lib.hku.hk/hkgro/view/g1879/685813.pdf
Hong Kong Government. (1880). Jury list for 1880. *The Hong Kong Government Gazette*. https://sunzi1.lib.hku.hk/hkgro/view/g1880/683620.pdf
Hong Kong Government. (1941). Jurors list for 1941. *The Hong Kong Government Gazette*. https://sunzi1.lib.hku.hk/hkgro/view/g1941/303089.pdf
Horan, J. (2012). *Juries in the 21st century*. Federation Press.
Hunter, J., & Crittenden, S. (2023). *The Australian jury in black & white: Barriers to Indigenous representation on juries*. Australasian Institute of Judicial Administration Incorporated. https://aija.org.au/wp-content/uploads/2023/08/Barriers-to-Indigenous-representation-on-juries.pdf
Iacobucci, F. (2013). *First Nations representation on Ontario juries*. https://turtletalk.files.wordpress.com/2013/02/english_fullreport.pdf
Johnson, L. D. (2016). What does justice have to do with interpreters in the jury room? *UMKC Law Review*, *84*(4), 941–985.
Judiciary. (2020, December). *Jury*. https:// www.judiciary.hk/en/jury/jury.html#2
Keskin, H., Arı, G., & Baştuğ, M. (2019). Role of prosodic reading in listening comprehension. *International Journal of Education and Literacy Studies*, *7*(1), 59–65. https://doi.org/10.7575/aiac.ijels.v.7n.1p.59
Kisor, C. (2001). Using interpreters to assist jurors: A plea for consistency. *Chicano-Latino Law Review*, *22*(1), 37–54.
Kramer, G., & Koenig, D. M. (1990). Do jurors understand criminal jury instructions? Analyzing the results of the Michigan Juror Comprehension Project. *University of Michigan Journal of Law Reform*, *23*(3), 401–438.
Kurita, T. (2012). Issues in second language listening comprehension and the pedagogical implications. *Accents Asia*, *5*(1), 30–44.
Landsman, S. (2002). Appellate court and civil juries. *Wisconsin Law Review*, *70*(3), 873–912.
Lau, C. (2017, September 27). Ex-Hong Kong leader Donald Tsang's trial about corruption at very top of government, prosecutors say – Male juror replaces woman on nine-member panel who could not pronounce 'verdict'. *South China Morning Post*.
Law Reform Commission of Hong Kong. (2010). *Report: Criteria for service as jurors*. https://www.hkreform.gov.hk/en/docs/rjurors_e.pdf
Law Reform Commission of Western Australia. (2010). *Selection, eligibility and exemption of jurors: Final report*. Law Reform Commission of Western Australia. https://www.wa.gov.au/system/files/2021-04/LRC-Project-099-Final-report.pdf
Law Reform Commission. (2010). *Consultation paper: Jury service* (LRC CP 61-2010). https://www.lawreform.ie/_fileupload/consultation%20papers/lrc%20juriescp%20full.pdf
Lee, C. W. (Director) (1996, February 8). *Peishen yuan* 陪審員 [*Jurors*] (TV series episode). Xinwen toushi 新聞透視 [News magazine]. Television Broadcasts Limited (TVB).

Leung, J. H. C. (2019). *Shallow equality and symbolic jurisprudence in multilingual legal orders*. Oxford University Press.

Library of Congress. (n.d.). *Magna Carta: Muse and mentor – Trial by jury*. https://www.loc.gov/exhibits/magna-carta-muse-and-mentor/trial-by-jury.html

Lloyd-Bostock, S., & Thomas, C. (1999). Decline of the 'Little Parliament': Juries and jury reform in England and Wales. *Law and Contemporary Problems*, *62*(2), 7–40.

Māori Language Act 1987, Pub. L. No. 176. (1987). https://www.legislation.govt.nz/act/public/1987/0176/latest/whole.html

McCann, M. (2017). No un jurado de mis pares: Juror exclusion of limited English proficient speakers. *The Scholar: St. Mary's Law Review on Race and Social Justice*, *18*(2), 346–377.

McKimmie, B. M., Antrobus, E., & Baguley, C. (2014). Objective and subjective comprehension of jury instructions in criminal trials. *New Criminal Law Review*, *17*(2), 163–183. https://doi.org/10.1525/nclr.2014.17.2.163

McSweeney, T. J. (2014). Magna Carta and the right to trial by jury. *William & Mary Law School Scholarship Repository*, *Faculty Publications*, *1722*, 139–157. https://scholarship.law.wm.edu/facpubs/1722

Mellinkoff, D. (1963). *The language of the law*. Little, Brown and Co.

Migration Policy Institute (2022). *New Mexico*. https://www.migrationpolicy.org/data/state-profiles/state/language/NM

Mikkelson, H. (2017). *Introduction to court interpreting* (2nd ed.). Routledge. https://doi.org/10.4324/9781315689586

Ministry of Justice. (2022, September 28). *Deaf jurors supported by sign language interpreter for first time*. GOV.UK. https://www.gov.uk/government/news/deaf-jurors-supported-by-sign-language-interpreter-for-first-time

Munn, C. (2001). *Anglo-China: Chinese people and British rule in Hong Kong 1841–1880*. Curzon.

Nakane, I. (2010). Partial non-use of interpreters in Japanese criminal court proceedings. *Japanese Studies*, *30*(3), 443–459. https://doi.org/10.1080/10371397.2010.518603

Nakane, I. (2016). Minority language speakers and disadvantage before the law: Challenges for applied linguistics. *Linguistics and the Human Sciences*, *11*(1), 9–29. https://doi.org/10.1558/lhs.v11i1.19060

Napier, J., & McEwin, A. (2015). Do deaf people have the right to serve as jurors in Australia? *Alternative Law Journal*, *40*(1), 23–27. https://pure.hw.ac.uk/ws/portalfiles/portal/8931251/2015_Napier_McEwin_Alt_LawJ.pdf

Napier, J., & Spencer, D. (2007). A sign of the times: Deaf jurors and the potential for pioneering law reform. *Reform: A Journal of National and International Law Reform*, *90*, 35–37.

Napier, J., & Spencer, D. (2008). Guilty or not guilty? An investigation of deaf jurors' access to court proceedings via sign language interpreting. In D. Russell & S. Hale (Eds.), *Interpreting in legal settings* (pp. 71–122). Gallaudet University Press.

Napier, J., & Spencer, D. (2017). Jury instructions: Comparing hearing and deaf jurors' comprehension via direct or mediated communication. *International Journal of Speech Language and the Law*, *24*(1), 1–29. https://doi.org/10.1558/ijsll.30878

Napier, J., Spencer, D., & Sabolcec, J. (2007). *Research report 14: Deaf jurors' access to court proceedings via sign language interpreting: An investigation*. NSW Law Reform Commission. https://lawreform.nsw.gov.au/documents/Publications/Other-Publications/Research-Reports/RR14.pdf

Napier, J., Spencer, D., Hale, S., Roque, M. S., Shearim, G., & Russell, D. (2018). Changing the international justice landscape: Perspectives on deaf citizenship and jury service. *Sign Language Studies*, *19*(2), 240–266. https://doi.org/10.1353/sls.2018.0034

New South Wales Law Reform Commission. (2007). *Jury selection* (117). New South Wales Law Reform Commission. https://www.parliament.nsw.gov.au/tp/files/26955/r117.pdf

New Zealand Law Commission. (1999). *Juries in criminal trials* (Preliminary Paper 37). Law Commission. https://www.nzlii.org/nz/other/nzlc/pp/PP37/PP37.pdf

New Zealand Law Commission. (2001). *Juries in criminal trials* (NZLC R69; Parliamentary Paper E 3169). New Zealand Law Commission. https://www.lawcom.govt.nz/assets/Publications/Reports/NZLC-R69.pdf

Ng, E. N. S. (2016). Do they understand?: English trials heard by Chinese jurors in the Hong Kong courtroom. *Language and Law / Linguagem e Direito*, *3*(2), 172–191.

Ng, E. N. S. (2018). *Common law in an uncommon courtroom: Judicial interpreting in Hong Kong*. John Benjamins. https://doi.org/10.1075/btl.144

Ng, E. N. S. (2020). Linguistic disadvantage before the law: When non-native English-speaking witnesses waive their right to an interpreter. In E. Ng & I. Crezee (Eds.), *Interpreting in legal and healthcare settings: Perspectives on research and training* (pp. 21–44). John Benjamins. https://doi.org/10.1075/btl.151.01ng

Ng, E. N. S. (2022). Trials heard by a foreign ear: A study of Chinese jurors' comprehension of English trials in Hong Kong. *International Journal of Speech, Language and the Law*, *29*(2), 172–200. https://doi.org/10.1558/ijsll.23248

Ng, E. N. S. (2023). The right to a fair trial and the right to interpreting: A critical evaluation of the use of *chuchotage* in court interpreting. *Interpreting. International Journal of Research and Practice in Interpreting*, *25*(1), 87–108. https://doi.org/10.1075/intp.00082.ng

Office of the Executive Secretary. (2023). *Virginia language access plan manual*. Department of Judicial Services. https://www.vacourts.gov/courtadmin/aoc/djs/programs/interpreters/manuals/lep/guidelines.pdf

Ogloff, J. R., & Rose, G. (2005). The comprehension of judicial instructions. In N. Brewer & K. D. Williams (Eds.), *Psychology and law: An empirical perspective* (1st ed., pp. 407–444). Guilford Press.

Ozolins, U., & Hale, S. (2009). Introduction. Quality in interpreting: A shared responsibility. In S. Hale, U. Ozolins, & L. Stern (Eds.), *The Critical Link 5: Quality in interpreting – a shared responsibility* (pp. 13–35). John Benjamins.

Pavlenko, A. (2008). 'I'm very not about the law part': Nonnative speakers of English and the Miranda warnings. *TESOL Quarterly*, *42*(1), 1–30. https://doi.org/10.1002/j.1545-7249.2008.tb00205.x

Pavlenko, A. (2021). Feigned incompetence: The pitfalls of evaluating Miranda comprehension in non-native speakers of English. *Language and Law / Linguagem e Direito*, *8*(1), 97–119. https://doi.org/10.21747/21833745/lanlaw/8_1a6

Pavlenko, A. (2023). Language proficiency as a matter of law: Judicial reasoning on Miranda waivers by speakers with limited English proficiency (LEP). *International Journal for the Semiotics of Law – Revue Internationale de Sémiotique Juridique*, *37*, 329–357. https://doi.org/10.1007/s11196-023-10037-8

Pavlenko, A., Hepford, E., & Jarvis, S. (2019). An illusion of understanding: How native and non-native speakers of English understand (and misunderstand) their Miranda rights. *International Journal of Speech Language and the Law*, *26*(2). https://doi.org/10.1558/ijsll.39163

Pavlenko, A., Hepford, E., Tavella, C., & Michalovic, S. (2020). Everyone has the right to understand: Teaching legal rights to ESL students. *TESOL Journal*, *11*(4). https://doi.org/10.1002/tesj.570

Piller, I. (2016). *Linguistic diversity and social justice: An introduction to applied sociolinguistics*. Oxford University Press. https://doi.org/10.1093/acprof:oso/9780199937240.001.0001

Pomerantz-Zhang L. (2012). *Wu Tingfang (1842–1922): Reform and modernization in modern Chinese history*. Hong Kong University Press.

Population Census Office. (2021). *Main results*. Census and Statistics Department, Hong Kong Special Administrative Region. https://www.censtatd.gov.hk/en/scode600.html

Ramirez, D. A. (1994). The mixed jury and the ancient custom of trial by jury *de medietate linguae:* A history and a proposal for change. *Boston University Law Review*, *74*(5), 777.

Rich, A. (2021). Bye, bye, bilinguals: The removal of English-Spanish bilinguals from the criminal jury and Latino discrimination. *Chicago-Kent Law Review Chicago-Kent Law Review*, *95*(3), 697–717.

Rickford, J. R., & King, S. (2016). Language and linguistics on trial: Hearing Rachel Jeantel (and other vernacular speakers) in the courtroom and beyond. *Language*, *92*(4), 948–988. https://doi.org/10.1353/lan.2016.0078

Ritter, J. L. (2004). Your lips are moving ... but the words aren't clear: Dissecting the presumption that jurors understand instructions. *Missouri Law Review*, *69*(1), 163–214.

Roberts-Smith, L. (2009). Forensic interpreting: Trial and error. In S. Hale, U. Ozolins, & L. Stern (Eds.), *The Critical Link 5: Quality in interpreting – a shared responsibility* (pp. 13–35). John Benjamins.

Scottish Courts and Tribunals Service. (n.d.). *Guide to jury service eligibility and applying for excusal*. https://www.scotcourts.gov.uk/coming-to-court/jurors/excusal-from-jury-service

Shuoshi ye cheng yingwen cha shen huomian dang peishen yuan bei ju 碩士也稱英文差 申豁免當陪審員被拒 [Request for exemption as juror by Master's degree holder based on poor English proficiency denied by court]. (2018, August 23). *Oriental Daily*. https://orientaldaily.on.cc/cnt/news/20180823/mobile/odn-20180823-0823_00176_036.html

Smith, C. T., & Munn, C. (2005). *Chinese Christians: Elites, middlemen, and the church in Hong Kong* (New ed.). Hong Kong University Press.

Smith, H. A. (2015). English language issues for jury service by New Zealanders from migrant and refugee backgrounds. *Kōtuitui: New Zealand Journal of Social Sciences Online*, *10*(1), 58–67. https://doi.org/10.1080/1177083X.2014.994535

Statistics Canada. (2021). *Census of population*. https://www12.statcan.gc.ca/census-recensement/index-eng.cfm?MM=1

Steele, W., & Thornburg, E. G. (1991). Jury instructions: Persistent failure to communicate. *Judicature*, *74*(5), 249–254.

Stern, L. (2012). What can domestic courts learn from international courts and tribunals about good practice in interpreting?: From the Australian war crimes prosecutions to the International Criminal Court. *T&I Review*, *2*, 7–30.

Thomas, C. (2008). Exposing the myths of jury service. *Criminal Law Review*, *415*, 1–10.

Thomas, C. (2010). *Are juries fair?* Ministry of Justice.

Thomas, C. A., & Balmer, N. J. (2007). *Diversity and fairness in the jury system*. Ministry of Justice. https://www.ucl.ac.uk/judicial-institute/sites/judicial-institute/files/diversity-fairness-in-the-jury-system.pdf

Tiersma, P. M. (1999). *Legal language*. University of Chicago Press.

Tiersma, P. M. (2008). The nature of legal language. In J. Gibbons & M. T. Turell (Eds.), *Dimensions of forensic linguistics* (pp. 7–25). John Benjamins Publishing Company. https://doi.org/10.1075/aals.5.03tie

Tiersma, P. M. (2009). Communicating with juries: How to draft more understandable jury instructions. *Loyola-LA Legal Studies Paper No. 2009–44*. http://papers.ssrn.com/sol3/papers.cfm?abstract_id=1507298

Trimboli, L. (2008). Juror understanding of judicial instructions in criminal trials. (Crime and Justice Bulletin No. 119). *NSW Bureau of Crime Statistics and Research*.

US Census Bureau (2022). *American community survey: 1-year estimates*. Census Reporter. http://censusreporter.org/profiles/04000US72-puerto-rico

United States Courts. (n.d.). *Juror qualifications, exemptions and excuses*. United States Courts. https://www.uscourts.gov/services-forms/jury-service/juror-qualifications-exemptions-and-excuses

Valentine II, A. L. (2015). My ears hear more than English: Granting multilingual jurors accommodations and treating multilingualism as a common type of juror expertise. *Boston College Law Review*, *56*, 1249–1285.

Wong, W. K. (2019). *The role of preparation using case-related materials in court interpreting*. [Unpublished doctoral dissertation], University of New South Wales. https://doi.org/10.26190/unsworks/21804

Wu, X., & Guo, M. (2022). Higher education expansion and the changing college wage premium in Hong Kong, 1976–2016. *Chinese Journal of Sociology*, *8*(1), 3–28. https://doi.org/10.1177/2057150X211073453

Legal references

Laws

British Sign Language Act 2022. https://www.legislation.gov.uk/ukpga/2022/34/contents/enacted

Contempt of Court Act 1981, c. 49. https://www.legislation.gov.uk/ukpga/1981/49

Coroners Ordinance, Cap. 504 § 42 (1) (1998). https://www.elegislation.gov.hk/hk/cap504

Criminal Code 1985, § 627. Justice Laws Website. https://laws-lois.justice.gc.ca/eng/acts/c-46/page-102.html#h-128409

Criminal Code, R.S.C. 1985, c. C-46, § 627. https://laws-lois.justice.gc.ca/eng/acts/C-46/section-627.html

Federal Court of Australia Act. (1976). *Eligibility for jury service and disqualification from jury service*. https://www.fedcourt.gov.au/going-to-court/jury/eligibility

Juries (Northern Ireland) Order 1996. https://www.legislation.gov.uk/nisi/1996/1141/schedule/2

Juries Act 1967, Australian Capital Territory. https://www.legislation.act.gov.au/a/1967-47/

Juries Act 1974, c. 23, § 1. https://www.legislation.gov.uk/ukpga/1974/23/section/1#reference-key-e2f07f271ea28cc708f470e32cb38d9d

Juries Act 1981, New Zealand. https://www.legislation.govt.nz/act/public/1981/0023/latest/whole.html

Juries Act 2000, Victoria. https://www.legislation.vic.gov.au/in-force/acts/juries-act-2000/059

Juries Act, RSO 1990. https://www.ontario.ca/laws/statute/90j03

Jury Act 1995, Queensland. https://www.legislation.qld.gov.au/view/whole/html/inforce/current/act-1995-042

Jury Act, RSBC 1996. https://www.bclaws.gov.bc.ca/civix/document/id/complete/statreg/96242_01#section4

Jury Act, RSNWT (Nu). (1988). https://canlii.ca/t/5217p

Jury Ordinance, Cap 3 § 24(3) (1999). https://www.elegislation.gov.hk/hk/cap3

Jury Ordinance, Cap 3 § 4(1c) (1999). https://www.elegislation.gov.hk/hk/cap3

Jury Selection and Service Act of 1968 ('JSSA'), 28 U.S.C. § 1865. (1968). https://uscode.house.gov/view.xhtml?path=/prelim@title28/part5/chapter121&edition=prelim

New Mexico Constitution. (1910). NM Const art. VII § 3 JUSTIA US Law. https://law.justia.com/constitution/new-mexico/article-vii/section-3/

US Const. amend. VI. Constitution Annotated. https://constitution.congress.gov/constitution/amendment-6/

United Nations. (1966). International Covenant on Civil and Political Rights. https://www.ohchr.org/en/professionalinterest/pages/ccpr.aspx

Court cases

Hernandez v. *New York* [1991] 500 U.S. 352, 358.

HKSAR v. *Chan Hon Wing* [2015] HCCC 210. https://legalref.judiciary.hk/lrs/common/search/search_result_detail_frame.jsp?DIS=104975&QS=%2B&TP=RS

HKSAR v. *Chan Hon Wing* [2020] HKCA 938. https://legalref.judiciary.hk/lrs/common/ju/ju_frame.jsp?DIS=131891

HKSAR v. *Chan Hon Wing* [2021] HKCFA 45. https://legalref.judiciary.hk/lrs/common/ju/ju_frame.jsp?DIS=141159&currpage=T

HKSAR v. *Chan Hon Wing* [2022] HKCFI 2426. https://legalref.judiciary.hk/lrs/common/search/search_result_detail_frame.jsp?DIS=146278&QS=%2B&TP=RS

HKSAR v. *Gutierrez Alvarez Keishu Mercedes* [2020] HKCA 184. https://bit.ly/42EVJHp

HKSAR v. *Henry Tse* [2016] HCCC 152.

HKSAR v. *Khaw Kim Sun* [2017] HCCC 374.

HKSAR v. *Lai She Hung* [2004] HCCC 184.

HKSAR v. *Lai She Hung* [2005] CACC 46. https://legalref.judiciary.hk/lrs/common/ju/ju_frame.jsp?DIS=46390&currpage=T

HKSAR v. *Moala Alipate* [2019] HKCA 537. https://bit.ly/42F89im

HKSAR v. *Tsang Yam Kuen Donald* [2015] HCCC 484.

Kinnally v. *R.J. Reynolds, et al.* [2023] 1684CV03937.

People v. *Guzman* [1984] 125 Misc.2d 457, 478 N.Y.S.2d 455. https://casetext.com/case/people-v-guzman-66

Regina v. *Christopher Huhne and Vasiliki Pryce* (*R.* v. *Pryce* 2013).

State of Florida v. *George Zimmerman* [2012] 592012CF001083A.

Structural Rubber Prods. Co. v. *Park Rubber Co.*, 749 F.2d 707, 713 (Fed. Cir. 1984).

United States v. *Cabrera-Beltran*, 660 F.3d 742, 748, 750 (4th Cir. 2011).

Weeks v. *Angelone* [2000] 528 U.S. 225.

Index

EU Authorised Representative:
Easy Access System Europe Mustamäe tee 50, 10621 Tallinn, Estonia
gpsr.requests@easproject.com

Printed and bound by CPI Group (UK) Ltd, Croydon, CR0 4YY
13/11/2025
01997476-0001